A Cabin on Great North Mountain

Earnest & Kate Mercer

First Edition

ISBN

13- 978-1460998755

10-1460998758

Publisher: Earnest B. Mercer

www.earnestmercerbooks.com

Florida

Printed in the United States of America

Dedication

Kate and Earnest dedicate this anecdotal recounting of the Mercer family's experiences atop Great North Mountain, Virginia to our children Brant and Deborah, and to our grandchildren, Lindsey, Kevin, Alex and Michelle.

Foreword

Those who hike, hunt, fish, camp, or dwell in secluded forests know that there are mischievous forces that live therein whose *raison d'etre*, it seems, is to play tricks, some playful, but most for making life miserable for human interlopers who venture into the domain of these woodland spirits. These forces are variously known as bandersnatchs by readers of Lewis Carroll, waldgeist by the Germans, trolls by the Norwegians, leprechauns by the Irish, gnomes in the Alps, and as gremlins by many Americans since WWII. The British RAF flyers first blamed gremlins as the culprits responsible for many malfunctions of their aircrafts without logical explanations. Since the war, gremlins have been reported far and wide over the United States. Though they are generally thought to be ugly green dwarf-like imps with short stubby horns and a constant malicious glint in their eyes, nobody has actually ever seen any. In all our years on Great North Mountain, we've never seen even one, but we know they are there. They have applied their mischief continually over the last thirty-eight years. While some of their pranks are comical, some are downright frustrating.

Setting

Great North Mountain is a part of the Shenandoah
Mountains, which are a part of the Allegany chain that lies
along the Virginia/West Virginia state line. Great North
Mountain is c. 2,500 feet above sea level and is covered in a
forest consisting mainly of chestnut oak, hickory and yellow
poplar trees. Kate and Earnest Mercer purchased seven
acres in the sparsely settled western side of Great North
Mountain and built a cabin nestled among the thick forest in
which a plethora of wildlife abounds.

Introduction

The authors, Earnest and Kate Mercer were lounging on the deck of the family cabin gazing into the forest below one summer's evening. The panorama that lay before them was of a healthy forest. The birds were darting in and out of the half-dozen feeders strung from overhead branches. A zephyr was soughing through the treetops and gently wafting down around them. Almost simultaneously, they glanced at each other and without a spoken word, acknowledged their contentment as they reminisced silently how it all came about.

Chapter I: The Search

Thirty-eight years before, in 1972, the Mercer family was camping in our Sears & Roebuck canvas tent in an idyllic setting on the bank of a mountain stream in upstate New York. At dusk, while we were relaxing around our campfire, a man drove into the site next to us pulling a shiny new camper on wheels. Once positioned, he pushed a button causing the canvas top to pop up, after which he proceeded to unload his gear. He started a gasoline generator positioned on the frame between the camper and his SUV. Next, he positioned a TV on a folding table and connected a cable to the generator. Then he settled into a folding chair and switched on the set. At that point, every member of our family affirmed our displeasure and acknowledged that this was the ultimate assault on our concept of camping in the wild.

We had been tent-camping for several years, always seeking the more primitive out-of-the way campgrounds; away from just the kind of annoyance that now spewed forth from the campsite right next door to us. We dearly loved the solitude of the state and national campgrounds, many of which date back to construction by the Civil Conservation Corps (CCC) during the Great Depression. But during recent trips, we had noticed that more of the wheeled camp vehicles were appearing where before only the less timid camping folk not averse to sleeping on the ground ventured. No longer could we enjoy communing with nature's woodland spirits without the annoying sounds that we had hoped to avoid.

We realized that we were unlikely to avoid the onslaught of the new wave of fainthearted campers, such as our neighbor in the next campsite, unwilling to forego television, cook on an open fire and sleep on the ground. After the episode with the camper and his noisy TV, powered by an equally intrusive gasoline generator, we decided to look for a place of our own that that could provide the solitude we sought. We longed for the chance to continue our connection with nature that we had enjoyed on earlier camping trips.

We retreated to the nearest indaba tree and held a family conference. Each of us expressed what we loved most about the woods and camping. That discussion yielded a set of priorities for us to pursue as we looked for our own property. First and most important, we wanted to find someplace in the midst of woodland surroundings that offered only the sounds of nature, away from motorized campers, gasoline generators, and portable televisions. We also gave a high ranking to a mountainous terrain, existing spring, lake or river, and a site within a six-hour drive from our present home in Rockland County New York.

Our search began by subscribing to catalogs specializing in rural property with the features we wanted. This was before computer listings were available. When we read about a likely place, we loaded our tent and headed for a campsite near the advertised property to use as a base for reconnaissance. But by the time we read about the property and arrived on the scene, it was usually sold. Still, we persevered.

Ranging near the limit of our six-hour driving distance we had decided on, we booked into The Cove, a private campground in Gore, a hamlet near Winchester, Virginia. While there, we admired the surrounding topography and asked the campground owner where we might find some similar land for sale. The friendly retired Navy Captain told us of a family that owned several hundred acres similar the campground on Great North Mountain, just a few miles away. He warned us that the owner of the land, Rolan Larrick, was particular about to whom he sold his property, and that we might consider his questions an infringement on our privacy. The Captain added that Mr. Larrick was an honest and a dependable man with whom to deal.

We immediately telephoned Mr. Larrick and set up a time to meet and discuss some land we might purchase from him. He asked numerous rather personal questions presumably to satisfy himself we were suitable candidates to share the land with the few people already there. Apparently comfortable with our responses, he agreed to show us an area that might fit our needs. We met him at the foot of Great North Mountain and began our search for a section of land we would like.

We parked our car, crowded into his vehicle, and labored up the mountainside via roads that really did not deserve that appellation. After jostling about half an hour, we stopped at the foot of a steep incline. The sixty-plus year old Mr. Larrick hopped spryly from his car and motioned for us to follow. That proved to be a challenge as he was agile as a gazelle and tireless. He led us to a parcel we could see immediately fell within most of our priorities. It was wooded, elevated, and fairly isolated from other property owners. A small stream ran along through the property. Our guide pointed out that the removal of a few trees would provide a good view of the valley.

We explained to Mr. Larrick that we hoped to obtain our water from a safe source so we wouldn't need to drill a deep-well, and asked him to show us the source of the stream. He agreed and we began a climb up the mountain. He commented along the way that the stream was fed by two small springs higher up the mountainside and that he had been drinking water from these springs for many years. That was good news.

As we scrambled up the mountainside, trying to keep up with the much older guide, we expressed our pleasure between gasps for oxygen. We liked the higher elevation and the apparent seclusion. Our little party soon reached the top of a knoll we'd been climbing and looked down on a ravine with a small stream coursing through it. Following Mr. Larrick's lead we started down the side of the ravine, happy to be going downhill for a change. Our breathing almost returned normal. Brant and Deb were close on the heels of Mr. Larrick seemingly not suffering as much from the exertion as were their parents.

So far, our jaunt through the woods had not encountered any threat from bugs, snakes, or other pests. But we knew from our camping experiences that little gremlins lurked in forests, behind trees and in bushes, awaiting a propitious time to exercise their mischievousness. We needed not to wait much longer for them to begin playing tricks on us. Just as we reached the edge of the flowing water, something—most likely the mountain gremlins— surreptitiously steered us into a yellowjacket nest.

Attacks by these nasty bees were not new to us as we had encountered them on previous outings. Those encounters served to establish a vivid awareness of their pernicious attacks and their painful stings. We knew yellowjackets to be aggressive and extremely protective of their nests. They will chase interlopers until danger to their home no longer exists. Unlike other members of the bee family, they don't lose their stinger with the first puncture, and will continue to sting time after time, often leaving a string of welts as they crawl along their victim's body.

Apparently our troupe had trespassed into their domain where there was probably an underground nest. Dozens of these nasty little buggers swarmed and attacked each of us, but seemed particularly drawn to Deb. She yelled like a banshee and scrambled up the other side of the streambed with me scurrying behind trying to beat the bees off her with my ball cap. When we had finally escaped, and could breathe again, I heard Mr. Larrick mutter under his breath something about waldgeists who had probably cost him a sale with their worrisome ways. We discovered some time later that waldgeists was the German name for puckish woodland gremlins.

Strangely, Brant escaped with only a couple of stings. He had avoided stings in past encounters with yellowjackets much to the consternation of the rest of us who could not understand why. Deb accused him of giving off an odor that kept the yellowjackets at bay; smelled something like uric acid, she said.

During the skirmish with the yellowjackets, we had crossed the stream without noticing its source being that we were occupied with other urgent matters at the time. When we reached the opposite top of the ravine, Mr. Larrick pointed out the two small springs he had referred to earlier as a source of good water. After we collected our wits, gone astray during the ordeal with the bees, we recognized the bluff on which we were standing was ideal for the construction of a small cabin that could be built overlooking the confluence of the two small streams originating from the springs, and in the distance, the West Virginia Mountains. Since we already knew that we were within the six-hour drive proviso, we were immediately convinced that spot was what we had been looking for; we had attained our objective.

We stopped lamenting the bee attack and asked Mr. Larrick if he could carve out a parcel that would include the bluff and both springs. He said he could do so, but cautioned that though one of the springs usually went dry during the late summer months, the other ran continuously. Even though the second spring slowed a great deal during periods with little rain, he said we could probably get drinking water from it. However, he cautioned, even the stream that continued to flow year round it was probably insufficient for general water usage without some means of capturing and storing an on-hand supply. We had no experience at converting a spring to a water supply for a cabin, but since my dad had put down many shallow wells in central Florida after his retirement, we hoped he might be able to help with the project. As we stood envisioning our retreat with a snug little cabin nestled amongst the trees on a bluff overlooking a pair of streams wending their way down the mountain, we didn't let a little detail like obtaining a supply of potable water for our dream cabin bother us.

We underestimated the enormity of the task that lay ahead before we could realize our dream, but the excitement at finally having our very own mountain cabin refuge overshadowed any doubts that arose.

Our daydreaming was interrupted by Brant's cry of "snake!" He was standing on a large boulder that would one day be in our front yard, and was pointing at a rattlesnake lying coiled at the base. Kate and I were familiar with the eastern diamondback rattlesnakes that inhabit Florida and *knew them to be mean tempered and extremely venomous,* so naturally we were alarmed and feared for our son's safety. Once fully aware of the   scenario, however, we saw that snake's proximity was not dangerous as long as Brant stayed on the boulder. Still, we remembered the time when we were on a camping trip in Mississippi and both Brant and Deb panicked when a snake swam toward the boat they were in and both leaped into a bayou infested with snakes. They swam to the bank, but I had to go into the water to fetch their abandoned boat as it drifted away. We shouted at Brant to not panic and stay on the rock where he was safe, all the while wondering what I would do if he freaked and jumped off the rock.

Unlike the eastern diamondbacks we remembered, this snake was relativity small and made no move to either attack or leave. Though it was coiled, it did not vibrate its tail and or give any other kind of warning. For a few moments that seemed like an eternity everybody in the group stood stock still. Then, with no hesitation Mr. Larrick killed the rattlesnake with a stick, all the while muttering something about how the mountain waldgeists were working overtime this day–first they had stirred up the yellowjackets, and now had placed a rattlesnake among us, probably intending to ruin his sale and drive us off the mountain.

We were tempted to ask him about the waldgeists; what they were, did they still dwell on the mountain, and should we be concerned with them, but he seemed in no mood to discuss the matter. Anyway, encounters with stinging bees and threatening snakes were not new phenomena to us. We had run across all sorts of animals while camping on primitive campsites; some were dangerous, some were just pests, and some were friendly. We accepted the presence of them all with equanimity. That's not to say, however, that to this day we don't have lingering memories of the episode with both the bees and the snake. We also recall his comments about waldgeists as they played their tricks on us in later days.

Mr. Larrick quoted us a price per acre and estimated that the section we wanted would survey out to between six and seven acres. We agreed on the price and made a down payment. After surveying the tract, he had a deed drawn up with date of sale as September 7, 1972.

We asked him about someone who could build us a cabin and help with outfitting it. He had constructed several cabins on the mountain, but was in the process of building one of his own and recommended we use a cabin-builder he knew to be reliable. We had designed the size and shape of what we wanted including a skin of aluminum to provide for a little more fire resistance. He contacted the man who specialized in mountain cabins and we let the contract with him. Mr. Larrick agreed to wire the cabin as he was a licensed electrician; he also said he would work as an intermediary for a small fee to arrange for the installation of plumbing and septic tank.

****

Like the true mountain man he was, Mr. Larrick loved the forests and mountains. As a young man, authenticating his Shawnee Indian heritage, he began spending most of his spare time on the mountain, and in 1932 he built his first cabin, a log structure which is still usable today. Being a jack-of-all-trades, he laid the foundation, cut and chinked the logs, installed the roof, and built a stone fireplace and chimney all without the use of power tools.

In later years when we began regular trips to the mountain, we'd slow the car and marvel at his old log cabin. By then, nobody had used the cabin for quite some time and it had fallen into disrepair. Because of its condition, Brant and Deb deduced the place was certainly haunted; it did look spooky. Like all good parents with a streak of mischievousness where young children are concerned, Kate and I embellished the haunted cabin image by pretending to occasionally see an apparition emerge from the chimney and hover until we passed. We softened the imaginary threat by explaining that the specter was probably "Casper the friendly ghost." For the next thirty-odd years, until the kids and later the grandkids, were too old for the pretense; we spoke to Casper each time we passed the old log cabin when they were with us. After so many years of carrying forth the myth, we began to wonder if there really was a mountain spirit living in the old log cabin. Maybe the waldgeist mentioned by Mr. Larrick lived there.

Chapter II: Building our Refuge

The plan Kate and I had sketched included two downstairs bedrooms with closets, a tiny bathroom, and a larger area with an open ceiling, a fireplace, and a sleeping loft that occupied one-half of the 20 x 30 ft. cabin. We planned for the loft to accommodate three single beds with storage space beneath the low lying slanted ceiling area on each side of the a-frame structure. At first the area could only be reached by a ladder, but later we replaced it with stairs, albeit not much easier to maneuver than the ladder. To this day, only the hale and hearty can reach the loft without a bit of trouble.

We did not plan for a heating system as we didn't plan to use the cabin in the winter, but we did order extra-heavy insulation with a moisture shield so that the interior would remain cooler in summer and warmer in colder months once we took the chill off using the fireplace.

The cabin was dried in and turned over to us by the builder in February 1973. It was only a shell with no amenities, but we had our cabin on Great North Mountain! Though it was only a skeleton of a cabin at the time, we loved it and looked forward to the challenge of converting it to our sanctuary from the noisy campers in their pop-up trailers, gasoline generators, TVs and other modern devices we considered unfit for the woodlands. From the very first, as we encountered unexplainable glitches, we began to suspect that the woodland spirits referred to by Mr. Larrick might be a little unhappy with our permanently invading their domain. That nagging suspicion remains, even to the current day.

****

By the following spring, the local power company had strung electric lines to the cabin and Mr. Larrick had connected electricity to the interior. Not long afterward my dad came up to volunteer his experience helping with the water supply to the cabin. He was accompanied by my mom and a couple of nephews. Dad brought a water pump designed to clear gravel from a well, a cold water tank, a concrete mixer, and other tools and supplies that he donated to the continued development of the cabin. The value of his contributions was inestimable.

My dad and I began to dig a cistern below the spring Mr. Larrick told us ran all year. We quickly found that digging in the shale mountainside was a herculean undertaking. There was little soil, but lots and lots of rocks so most common digging tools were ineffective. It became a task of breaking loose the shale and digging the pieces out by hand. But with the use of the gravel pump, we were able to spew out the smaller pellets of rock and create a hole large enough to trap a small supply of water.

We threaded a flexible PVC pipe and an electric line overland through the trees and shrubs from the site of the spring to the cabin. Next, we installed a water tank beneath the cabin floor and connected the PVC pipe and electric wire. When that was done, the cabin had a meager water supply, but the plumbing was not usable. A septic system had yet to be installed. An electric stove and some kitchen cabinets had been put in place, so we had lighting and cooking facilities.

My dad and I were pleased with our progress on the water supply, but our good fortune was about to run out. The remnants of a dying tropical storm arrived, stalled overhead, and began to dump a heavy rain on the mountain. The downpour lasted for seven days and seven nights straight; the streams grew into raging torrents, sometimes five or six feet high! We suspected that the valley and surrounding areas were flooded, probably making all area roads and bridges including those on Great North Mountain unusable. We were stranded on the mountain with no means of communication as a telephone line had not been installed and cellular phones were a thing of the future.

The family group of eight people was confined to the shell of a cabin and my parents' small camper. We were crowded, but faced no immediate threat. We had brought bunk beds for Brant and Deb, a double bed for us from our home in New York, and my parents had brought an extra single mattress for the upstairs loft. Mom and dad slept in their camper. Kate and I slept in the double bed, and the youngsters slept in the loft.

The improvised water cistern provided a pittance supply for our use, but we had lots of running water—from the deluges pummeling us from the sky or from the rampaging streams. Since we didn't have workable indoor plumbing and we knew that the camper's tiny bathroom would be overwhelmed with the use by eight people, I knew I had to improvise. I constructed a one-hole privy using the packing material from our kitchen appliances. It sat in all its splendor of bright red, white and blue cardboard at the edge of the cabin clearing and stood out from the surrounding woods like a patriotic monument.

Actually I was quite proud of the architectural symmetry of the colorful privy. The cabin occupants were ecstatic with the prospect of not having to "go" with buckets of water falling on them from the sky. Even though the cardboard began to sag and separate in places, it kept the rain off the users during the entire storm! It served us until we could get a septic system installed much later.

So, we had plenty of water, a place to relieve ourselves in relative privacy, and fortunately we had enough food to weather the storm. We could cook inside the cabin, and during sporadic power outages, my mother cooked hot dishes on her gas powered camper stove. We also had a pump-up gasoline camp stove for emergencies. Be often made do with cold sandwiches and food taken directly from cans. My parents had brought two Kerosene lamps as gifts; we put them to good use after dark when there was a loss of electric power. We still have the Kerosene lamps, and have used them from time to time over the years. We also have the gasoline camp stove as well.

Even though we were managing quite well in view of the circumstances, my dad worried constantly. He was the worrying type; sometimes he worried about not having anything to worry about. He paced the floor like a caged animal, not really knowing what he was so concerned about. Once, he donned his improvised shower cap he had made from a plastic bag and slogged all the way down to Back Creek at the bottom of the mountain to satisfy himself that he was indeed captive of the elements. When the rain finally stopped, he was champing at the bit to get off the mountain and head for Florida; not so much because he was so unhappy with being on the mountain, or that he needed to get home for any specific reason, but just because he could not bear the thought of being marooned.

After my parents and the tagalong nephews pulled out, Kate and I took stock of our mountain sanctuary: the desolation left by the storm, our failure to develop an adequate water supply, the enormous effort needed to complete the interior of cabin, and the task of finding craftsmen to do the work we could not do ourselves. For the first time we felt a trace of uneasiness at the colossal task that lay ahead of us and wondered if we had bitten off more than we could chew. The can-do spirit that invigorated us in the beginning flagged. We were aware of Murphy's Law, "whatever can go wrong, will", and we suspected that it might also be the mantra of the woodland spirits.

****

The stream we chose for our water supply was inadequate and the water we managed to pump to the cabin contained too much silt to be of much use. We had to find an alternative, but what? We were adamantly opposed to a deep well if there was any possible alternative. We heard that the water from existing deep wells lower down the mountain was not nearly as pure and tasteful as the natural spring water, besides there was the expense. Some wells required several attempts, probing deeper and deeper before acceptable water was found, with costs running into the hundreds upon hundreds of dollars.

Over the next few visits to the cabin, the flow of the spring continued, but ever so slowly and my makeshift cistern was a failure. I lost confidence that I could ever trap enough water for general use in the cabin, or that I could keep silt and other debris out of the flow.

The spring in the other ravine continued to produce a flow as well, actually creating a stream with a greater volume than its counterpart. Mr. Larrick's caution that it dried up in the summer had discouraged my consideration as a good source. But as I studied the situation, I saw that the stream fell away at more than a foot per meter at one point as it made its way down the mountain. I could see a spot where the topography would accommodate a cistern large enough for our needs without having to dig through the almost impenetrable shale rock bed. But, how would I channel the flow into such a cistern? I had not yet located the spring itself.

I laboriously dug through the forest debris accumulated above the only water I could see coming from the mountainside, searching for the main source of the flow. After some hard work, I eventually found that water continuously flowed from a crevice in a rock on the side of the mountain about twelve feet up the ravine. The water flowing from the crack in the rock ran downhill to the place I thought I might possibly build an adequate cistern. The rate of flow from the spring was not great, but I figured that with a sizable cistern, I could entrap enough water to meet our daily needs, though I worried that I would not have enough reserve to combat a fire, should the need arise. We were so far from a fire station and at the end of almost inaccessible roads; we knew that we were in the hands of a greater power.

I still faced the problem of channeling the flow from the source into a catchment tank. Hopeful that I had solved our water supply dilemma, I jammed a short length of pipe into the hole from which the water was running and watched for several minutes as a non-stop stream of clear mountain water free of debris flowed from the pipe. For once, Mr. Larrick's waldgeist did not thwart my efforts. When I was reasonably comfortable that the spring was constant, I connected a twelve-foot PVC pipe to the short piece I'd already stuck into the mountainside and channeled the output to the place where I could build a reservoir.

My cistern-building skills were minimal at best. All I had to work with was a general concept of such a project and my extraordinary, though often misplaced, self-confidence. Some of the obstacles were truly daunting. The place for the floor of the cistern was steep, heavily ridged with bedrock, and continuously covered by a thin flow of water. How could I pour concrete on such a surface? How could I stem the flow of water so I could construct the walls of the tank? How would I be able to keep debris out of the tank? How would I be able to get the mortar and concrete blocks I intended to use down the mountainside? These challenges kept me awake for much of the ensuing nights.

The first thing I managed to do was divert the water flow with rocks, leaves, and some kaolin clay from a nearby deposit. Kaolin clay, used in pottery, proved to be suitable for stopping holes and cracks in my makeshift dam. I rigged a block and tackle mounted on a steel cable connected to trees near the cabin and the spring. My dad, who had returned to help me, mixed the mortar and sent it and the blocks down using the cable and a bucket attached to the block and tackle.

I eventually constructed a concrete block cistern that could hold about 90 gallons of water and a platform to hold an electric water pump. Then, I ran electric wire and PVC pipe overland 100 feet up the side of the ravine and beneath the cabin foundation where I replaced the connections to the other spring with those of the new supply. (Little did I know that the in-house gremlin had some unpleasant plans for me in its bag of tricks relative to the transfer of electric power from one pump station to another. But that comes later.)

My first cistern consisted of four walls, a poured concrete floor and a sheet of plywood over the top to help keep debris out. The walls began to collapse after a few years, and the plywood top proved inadequate for keeping surface water and trash out. My self-confidence wavered. By continuously making repairs and cleaning debris from the catchment, we used it on our occasional visits for several months until I became completely exasperated with the collapsing walls and rotting plywood top; not to mention finding all sorts of unwanted flora and fauna in the water from time to time. Eventually, facing reality vis-a-vis my reservoir building skills, or lack thereof, I decided what was needed was a large self-contained tank of some kind that would keep the collected water clean.

During a later visit by Brant, we scoured the county for a supplier of the kind of tank we wanted. Finally we located a company that sold us an 85 gallon plastic tank that we could cut holes in for the necessary connections. We installed the tank within the deteriorating walls of the cement block cistern, hoping that what was left of the old walls would protect the new tank from falling tree limbs and inquisitive animals. We fashioned snug holes in the plastic to accommodate the intake pipes from the flow in the crevice in the rock above and for a pipe to the pump and on to the pressure tank at the cabin. Then we cut a drain hole near the downstream bottom of the container to use for periodic draining of the silt that would collect from the flow. Later, I constructed an a-frame plywood cover to further protect the system. The plastic tank has not only made the cistern impervious to surface water, critters, and other undesirables, but has worked better and has lasted for more than twelve years at this writing.

The spring has faithfully flowed for 38 years, through rainy seasons and dry spells. There have been times during draughts when the supply flowing into the cistern was reduced to a trickle and it was necessary to restrict our water usage by less time in the shower and by not using the garden hose for watering. During these long dry spells, neighbors' deep wells sometimes dried up or the water became muddy. On at least one occasion during a prolonged dry period, a nearby family, obtained drinking water from our spring and carried back to their home in jugs because their deep well could not supply clean water.

We eventually installed a whole house water filter which removed silt down to five microns. One year the kids took a bottle of this spring water to school show-and-tell where it was judged to be the best tasting water of the samples brought in by other students.

****

Out of necessity, I learned many skills over the years besides how to install a water supply. Because of the limited space in our 20 X 30, cabin Kate and I conjured up space savings devices and concepts. We made a modified Murphy-bed that hangs from the wall in Kate's china painting studio so we can sleep one more person if other beds are occupied. It was originally constructed to provide granddaughter, Lindsey, with privacy in her early teen years.

The kitchen area has very limited counter space so together we dreamed up more space-saving ideas. I built a bar for mixing drinks. It hangs from the wall like a miniature Murphy-bed, and when closed takes up only six inches of space. The door opens on hinges to make a mixing counter. With a few attachments, it also became a home for cocktail and wine glasses, coffee mugs, espresso cups, swizzle sticks, and even a place for our telephone/address book.

Another trick we applied to save space was to saw certain inside doors in half and attach hinges so that we could fan-fold them out of the way. When we needed a microwave oven, we hung it from the wall to save counter space; we even installed a homemade breadbox over the oven for the same reason.

Plans for the cabin called for only small closets in the bedrooms, so I built two armoires to accommodate clothing and one for Kate's art supplies and other stuff. By placing a shelf between the two clothing armoires in the bedroom and building a stool, it serves as a dressing table for Kate. When the cabinet I built for Kate to store her china painting materials and other stuff proved to occupy too much space, I sawed it in half vertically leaving an armoire only 14 inches deep. When we needed some end tables, I made them with unmatched legs; one side straight, the other side slanted, so that they could be placed snuggly against their respective chairs to save space. I constructed several bookshelves, also made with space saving in mind; and then built a corner shelf to hold the TV and DVD player leaving space beneath for my recliner.

Brant, Kate and I learned the questionable "art" of hanging paneling. The builder did not seal the inside of the cabin, so we installed paneling throughout, walls and ceiling. Handling the 4 X 8 sheets of paneling was awkward and required the six hands of three people and Deb's subjective supervision. A carpet outlet store provided us with carpeting that Brant and I installed wall to wall over the subflooring left by the builder rather than other forms of floorcovering. Carpeting was easier for us and less expensive.

Over time I learned how to solder copper plumbing, how to maintain electrical systems, and how to lay field stone for a chimney, hearth and other projects such as retaining walls, etc. Few people consider the fact that when atop a mountain and miles from the nearest Lowes or Home Depot, one must improvise. For that reason, I never discard anything that I think might have some future use, no matter how obscure the use may be at the time. Many times, a selection from my "junk" collection has saved the day.

The original cabin design that Kate and I drew called for a stone chimney. After much of the essential fitting-up inside the cabin had been done, we set about building our chimney. At first, we asked around for someone with experience to build the structure for us, but finding nobody interested, we boldly (foolishly?) decided to attempt the job ourselves. First we needed building material, so we drove our pickup truck up and down the mountain roads and collected suitable field stones, hauled them back to the cabin and stacked them for use when we started the chimney. Gathering and transporting the stones was backbreaking work, and later hoisting them to lay in layers to form the chimney was no easier task for us. Some stones we chose were too heavy for us to pick up, so I constructed a kind of sled—two wooden runners with a platform on top—a contrivance I remembered from my boyhood, when folks in Alabama would use such a device to haul fertilizer and such to the fields. The sled was pulled by a mule in those days. Having no mule available on the mountain, I used my Mazda truck. When the electric company discarded an anchor line after having run electricity to the cabin, I of course saved the 20-foot piece of steel cable, just in case I might need it one day. I retrieved the cable from my junk pile and attached one end to the chassis of our pickup truck and the other to the makeshift sled. Kate and I rolled the heavier stones we couldn't lift onto the sled and then rolled them off back at the cabin. We must have made a comical picture, pulling a homemade wooden sled with a huge rock on it behind an old pickup truck along the mountain roads. Once we had a store of such stones, we began the construction of a chimney twenty-two feet high, six feet wide, and three feet deep. Mr. Larrick had cast a footing and laid concrete blocks around the Orangeburg flue, so our job was made easier by just fitting stones around the block substructure.

After laying the first few layers of stone, I rigged a block & tackle to raise the remaining stones up to me as the work proceeded upward. Kate's job was to roll the stones onto a cradle and hoist them up to me on the scaffolding. The rig enabled her to send up stones heavier than she could lift, but every now and then, her zeal overshadowed her strength. In these instances, she would give a great heave on the pulley holding the cradle with a super heavy stone, only to have the cradle and stone drop back down to the ground. Doggedly refusing to let go of the line, she took a short, but hasty trip up the scaffolding. The weight of the stone would lift her 100-pound body into midair. When this happened I'd leave the scaffolding, raise the stone to the level of work, tie off the pulley line, and crawl back on the scaffolding to place the stone in its place. We enjoyed a good belly laugh at the spectacle of Kate hoisting up the stone only to pass it by as it returned to the ground. This still brings a smile to us when we talk about the image of Kate sailing through the air tethered to a rope.

Since much of the chimney work was done on weekends and holidays, we inevitably returned to our New Jersey home with sore and aching muscles that healed after a few days only to be stressed next trip. Nevertheless, the hard work was a labor of love. We toiled on the chimney for the next three years during trips to the cabin. I'm sure the chimney would not win architectural awards, but we think it's gorgeous, and it works like a charm.

When the chimney was finished, my "Dutch Uncle", Mr. Larrick, gave us some tips on laying a stone hearth. We found a supply of natural slate deposited in the confluence of two streams at the bottom of the mountain and harvested enough of the beautiful flat rock to make a top for our hearth. Later we used more of the slate to top off a walkway leading from the back clearing to the cabin deck. We obtained a large slab of American Black Walnut wood from the "tree man" in Cranbury NJ, where we lived at the time. I shaped the beautiful piece of wood into a fireplace mantle and Kate polished it to a gleaming beauty before we mounted it above the hearth. I found an iron rod about three feet long, heated the end to mold a hook and used it as a poker. We obtained an ash remover from a smithy on a trip to North Carolina. A child's play broom served as a fireplace broom.

Over the years, we collected various accouterments from yard sales; those that fit with the cabin "décor". Much of the other furnishings, I either made from scratch or refurbished from pieces from garage sales. Our first fridge came from a used furniture store. The small refrigerator was 50 years old when we bought it and it lasted several years before we bought a replacement and gave the old one to our neighbor. It functioned for many years after that.

We also bought from a yard sale two old weather-beaten hanging lamps which we still use today

****

Kate, a great lover of plants and flowers, wanted to create a small garden with a pool and a bird bath in the yard so she could watch the birds drinking and bathing amid a display of colorful blossoms. After building the chimney, no task was beyond our inflated know-how, so I began to scrounge about for materials to accomplish her vision. I remembered that when we moved the water source from one spring to another, I did not remove the electric wire and PVC pipe I had installed there. It had been easier to lay new wire and pipe to the other spring than retrieve the older ones buried under rock and soil. So, to build Kate's "oasis", I planned to locate the buried electric wire and use it to run a small water pump in the pool yet to be constructed. The ever vigilant gremlin must have been perched on an overhead limb smirking with gleeful expectations as I searched for the wire I had buried several years before. I dug exploratory hole after exploratory hole before finally finding the wire nearly ten feet from where I thought it should have been. More smirking from the little green imp, but I reveled in the fact that I had thwarted the mischievous midget monster one more time. But the imp did not give up and had the last laugh when much to my pain and humiliation, a jolt from 240 volts of electricity projected me several feet through the air. I had forgotten to disconnect the line from its power source beneath the cabin when I abandoned the earlier water supply.

After belatedly making sure that the wire was not live, I cut it and connected it to an electric box I installed near the pool site so the fountain pump could be plugged in. Then I rigged a switch inside the porch so the fountain could be turned on or off without going outside. I located an old Rubbermaid container in my junk pile that Kate said would be suitable for the pond. After we dug a pit, installed the Rubbermaid receptacle, laid rocks around the upper perimeter, installed a water pump and a "spitting" frog, we turned on the power. Voile! Kate had her little homemade oasis in the cabin yard. She promptly began to plant a variety of flowers.

Each summer on arriving, one of her first chores is to obtain and plant a new crop of annuals. It has been a great pleasure over these many years to watch the birds visit the fountain for a drink or bath, the butterflies that visit the blossoms, and to see a humming bird stick its long tongue in a bloom for a sip of nectar. Observing a goldfinch stop by in all its splendor with the green of the forest in the background is justification enough for the work required to build the fountain (and coincidentally my short flight through the air provided courtesy of the 240V 60 amp. current.). The deer and sometimes a bear come by for a drink as well.

****

We have used native stone for numerous projects including: a stone walkway, a stone pump house at the spring supplying our water, a stone barbeque pit (also used as an incinerator to burn household trash not recyclable) and Kate's own objet d'art gracing a stone patio. This creation by Kate is made from a composite sedimentary rock balanced on other common sandstone rocks, creating a kind of rudimentary Japanese lantern. I found the unusual conglomerate stone in the creek bed and Kate thought it would be a neat decoration. The *objet d'art* was created as a joke, but we liked it enough to maintain it over the last 20 years or so. Sometimes on arrival, we find the rocks jumbled into a pile and the sediment rock, which is round, way down in the forest where it has rolled after someone or something knocked it over; most likely a pesky gremlin.

****

A couple of years ago, Kate and I began collecting large stones to build a retaining wall alongside the creek leading from our cistern. We wanted to stop the erosion. The stones were so heavy, we had to lift them together, and some we had to roll. They lay by our wood pile near the cabin for several months awaiting help to get them down to the creek and lay them on the slope between our picnic/bird-watching bench and the creek. Eventually, Brant and Alex, responding to the insistent urging from "Granny", moved the stones to the site via the cable and cradle we had used in the construction of the water supply several years before.

They began constructing the wall, eventually using all the stones we had on hand. Kate and I finished after the "boys" left using additional stones we harvested from the mountainside.

Once Granny gets a project into her vision, there is no let up until it's done, and though it took almost two years to accomplish, she is happy with the results and that's what counts. She has been the driving force behind making the cabin comfortable and attractive.

****

We've also built and placed several wood benches at choice bird watching spots in the area near the cabin and hung several bird feeders from nearby trees. We often take a sandwich and drinks to one of these benches to watch for birds and absorb the delightful aura of woodlands as we munch our lunch. And sometimes, we pack fare and hike into the woods until we find an attractive place to picnic.

****

The bears, raccoons and flying squirrels target feeders we hang on the trees on a regular basis. To foil the bears' efforts, I tied cords to rocks and hurled them over high branches; some more than thirty feet above ground, and fastened feeders to the other end out of reach of the marauding bruins. However, this tactic did not always stop the masked robbers and flying rodents that seemed to find ways to get to the feeders no matter how high I tied them. I'm convinced that without their aid from my little green enemies, the gremlins, I could outwit the raccoons and flying squirrels, but Kate is not so sure. The battle goes on.

Sometimes after dark or when waking during the night, we would shine our high-powered flashlights on and below the bird feeders, occasionally catching the raccoons and flying squirrels during their raids. Once we caught a bear sow with a yearling cub munching seeds that the other animals had sloshed out of the feeder. As an aside, we found out by accident that the flying squirrels are descendants of ancestors that date to the ice age and are extremely rare. We didn't see the lovable creatures for more than twenty years after settling in the cabin; then they came in numbers exceeding a dozen; but their numbers have declined significantly in the last two years. We don't know why.

Recently a family of raccoons had been pillaging a feeder that is hung over fifteen feet above ground from a slender branch no bigger than an index finger. One of the nimble and crafty creatures shinnied out on the bough and grabbed the cord holding the feeder, thereby creating a sling-shot effect which caused the feeder to spill its contents on the ground where the rest of the family is waiting. I think the gremlins taught them this trick. Kate thinks I'm crazy.

****

Several years after the cabin was complete, Kate and I decided we needed more room so I sketched out a design for a screened porch that was to be attached on the side of the cabin next to the chimney. It was to be ten feet deep and twenty feet long, reaching from the back of the cabin to abut the stone chimney.

Brant was scheduled to come up one summer and before he came, I built some concrete block pillars and ordered the building materials. Neither Brant nor I had much carpentry experience, but we had lots of self-confidence, maybe an excess.

On his arrival, we set about the project without the least hesitation. First we laid the joists and put in a plywood floor, and then we built the walls and hoisted them into place. Next, we attached 2 X 8 rafters to the existing cabin rafters and affixed them to the walls we had erected. We covered the structure with plywood and later installed vinyl shingles on top of the plywood roof. After sealing the whole structure with more plywood, we declared the project finished for that summer. Later on we installed linoleum over the plywood floor and with the help of grandson Alex ran electric wiring to strategic spots for lamps, etc. Then Alex helped me install screen wire windows and a screen door. Finally, a following summer, I installed decorative plywood, called 10-11, I think, on the outside walls over the construction grade we had used and stained it redwood to match the aluminum siding of the cabin. We furnished the porch with a sofa bed that provides sleeping accommodations for two more people, a homemade dining table, overhead fans, and several lamps. I also added a cubicle for my computer. Often, especially during rains, we lounge on the sofa and watch the rain falling on the nearby trees and listen to the patter on the roof—very soothing and satisfying. But, due to my nature, I often sit on the porch and instead of admiring our accomplishments, pick out the mistakes we amateur carpenters made. Doing so is a disconcerting habit of mine relative to almost any project I undertake.

Now that Kate and I approach our dotage, almost everything we wanted done is completed in our refuge on the mountain, all that remains is the repairs and maintenance, with which thankfully, our son and grandsons are quite willing to assist.

Chapter III Animals We Have Known

Sometime, many years ago, a pair of flycatchers with the eponymous name Phoebe built a nest on a tall chestnut oak tree. Generation after generation, these graceful and useful birds returned to nest in the same tree. They caught untold thousands of insects and filled the woods with their call. In 1973, we interrupted this longstanding ritual. Unaware of the phoebe's custom, we picked the spot for our cabin where their nesting tree had stood for many years. The builder uprooted the tree to lay foundation. Later, when the cabin walls and roof were completed, but not the doors and windows, the phoebes seeking their ancestral home found a man-made structure in its place. Their tree was gone so they built their nest on the exact spot they had fledged their young for generations, but this time on a 2 x 8 rafter hewn from a distant tree. After the fledging, we moved the now vacant nest to a spot on the outside eave of the cabin and hoped the phoebes wouldn't mind the slight shift in its location. They didn't, and for many years thereafter the delightful little creatures nested beneath the roof overhang of the cabin. Year after year the little birds returned. Then, two years in a row, something, we couldn't determine what, destroyed their nest before their young could fledge. They haven't returned and we sorely miss them.

****

Not long after occupying the cabin, we spotted an entrance hole beneath a huge boulder from which Brant had spied the timber rattler on our initial inspection of the property. We kept watch on the entrance for a long time before we were finally able to identify the small animal that lived in the hole. It was a mink. The sleek little animal, in its summer coat of reddish-brown lived under the boulder for several years. Being a nocturnal animal, we saw it only when we stayed up at night with a light and patiently waited, but the evidence around the entrance to the den testified to its continued usage. After several years, the den showed little evidence of usage. But in 2010, I found the entranceway cleared of debris indicating either the mink or some other denizen used the burrow. According to our research, the mink has several "cousins" living on the mountain: martins, weasels, ferrets, et al. We don't usually see them during our summer visits, but we do see occasional signs indicating their presence.

We found another entranceway to an underground den, this time beneath the poured concrete footing of the cabin. We were concerned that the inhabitant's tunneling might weaken the foundation, so I blocked the entrance with some rocks. The next morning the rocks had been removed. Each day I blocked the entrance and each night something cleared it away. This recurring ritual continued off and on during our periodic visits for several months. We joked that this must be where the woodland imps of Mr. Larrick's lamentations live. Joke? Well we had no idea what did live in the dark recesses of the burrow. Then early one morning just after dawn, we saw a bizarre spectacle on the cabin deck. A large male raccoon that had been visiting from time to time looking for tidbits that we left for him was standing stock still glaring at what looked much like a black and white dust mop. It wasn't a dust mop at all, but a strange little animal standing on four legs so short as to appear there were none. Its broad back was black with numerous white spots forming no particular pattern. The two forest denizens just stood immobile and glared at each other; the raccoon with a low growl and his adversary with an occasional hiss. The standoff lasted for several minutes allowing us time to consult our animal guide book. We found the strange creature unmistakably illustrated. It was a spotted skunk, sometimes called a civet cat. While we had at first been concerned that the larger raccoon might attack and harm his smaller adversary we now wondered if the raccoon knew what he was setting himself up for. According to our guide book, the spotted skunk's scent glands are as potent as its larger cousin, the striped skunk.

Eventually the raccoon, clever animal that he was, backed away from the confrontation and retreated down the stairs off the deck. After waiting for a few minutes, the little skunk casually waddled off the deck on its nearly invisible legs, and descended by the opposite stairs to the burrow under the foundation. Neither animal was the worse for the encounter. We admired the little skunk's courage in its face off with the much larger raccoon, and thereafter as a tribute to its pluck we did not disturb the access to its den. The cabin foundation has not collapsed and the den is still there 38 years later. Spotted skunks only venture out at night, so we haven't seen one for a long time, though the entranceway is kept clear, even when I place small rocks over it to confirm a resident. Over such a long time, there must have been at least three or four generations living in the lair.

****

When Deb was a junior in high school, her curriculum included a French class. As part of a cultural exchange, she hosted a student from France. Thierry spoke very little English. Deb, of course, could speak some French, but the rest of the family kept an English-French dictionary handy. Thierry winced at my annihilation of the French pronunciation, but we had fun and got along well. Thierry was a good sport and we had many lively exchanges over the dinner table.

We decided that a trip to our cabin would be a treat for the French boy. He was a city dweller and said he had little chance to visit forests in France. He eagerly looked forward to the trip. Once we had arrived at the cabin, Thierry was ecstatic at being in the American "wilderness". One day, we hiked up to the very top of the mountain, accompanied by our dog, a Whippet named Bleau. Thierry was surprised but quite pleased at our choice of a French name for our pet. We explained to Thierry as best we could that Bleau was a city dog and had no more experience in the woodlands than he. Bleau loved the woods and often entertained herself with scaring up various small game. But Bleau, and most whippets, are excitable and once she discovered another animal she could become uncontrollable.

We walked to the top of Great North Mountain where a spur of the Appalachian Trail runs along the crest. One direction leads to the Shenandoah Boy Scout camp, the other way passes Pinnacle Rock, the highest point of the mountain, and eventually enters the George Washington National Forest seventeen miles away. We hesitated while deciding which direction we would hike, since one direction ran along an escarpment of huge rocks deposited by the Ice Age glazier that created the mountain range and was somewhat more challenging than the other way, but more varied and interesting. The other direction was more deeply forested and sloped gently up to Pinnacle Rock before falling away toward the National Forest.

As we took a breather and cogitated on our next move, a humongous striped skunk came ambling by about twenty yards away, seemingly oblivious of its surroundings, including the party of human trespassers. The skunk was a boar that, judging from his appearance, had lived long and been through a lot. His fur was long and scraggly, tinged with gray. He was covered in mountain dust and his posterior was stained from many times expelling his defense musk.

Apparently, neither Thierry nor Bleau was aware of what the skunk was capable of doing for its own protection. Bleau sprinted after the old brute, and apparently driven by our shouts to cease and desist, Thierry became concerned for the dog's safety and chased after her. The scenario was comical even with the prospect of a disastrous outcome. "Mr. Pepe la Phew", nicknamed after the popular cartoon skunk, was in the lead, Bleu was closing in, and Thierry was about five or six yards behind. Old "Pepe" tired quickly of all the nonsense behind him and let loose with his own personal eau de perfume that saturated both boy and dog causing them to stop dead in their tracks. They struggled to find a way to breathe while enveloped in a cloud of pungent, stifling, and horribly smelly spray while the old boar nonchalantly continued his ambling gait into the woods.

Now what, we thought? We didn't know whether to laugh or cry. The odor was so strong we could hardly stand approaching either Thierry or Bleau. We somehow managed to put a leash on Bleau without suffocating, and asked Thierry to hold on to it. As we began our descent for the cabin, we motioned for Thierry to follow a few yards behind us. Once back, we instructed Thierry to strip and shower immediately. Luckily, we had provided him with some of Brant's old clothes for the hike, so we just burnt them on the spot. Tending Bleau was a different matter. We tried every trick we knew including the suggested remedy of tomato juice to eliminate Mr. Pepe la Phew's eau de cologne; nothing worked. Even several months later, if Bleau's fur got damp the old skunk's legacy spun an odiferous aura around the hapless dog. Maybe the skunk was really our nemesis the gremlin in disguise?

Thierry was mortified. He explained that he had been very concerned for the safety of Bleau and did not stop to think that "Pepe" would spray them. We don't know how Thierry coped with the smell on his trip back to France, but hoped he did not get evicted from the airplane he took back home. We did not see Thierry again, but every time we see a striped skunk, we think of him and his initiation to the "American wilderness". His parting gift from us was a miniature porcelain skunk!

****

I think snakes are detested by most humans, perhaps because they get such a bad rap in the biblical story of the Garden of Eden. Great North Mountain is the home of several species of these reptiles including timber rattler and copperheads, neither of which is a threat to humans if reasonable care is taken. Both are venomous, but not particularly aggressive. Perhaps the most populous snakes on the mountain are several species of blacksnake. They grow to great size and with their shiny black skin and piercing eyes can be quite startling to the unwary individual that happens to come upon one unexpectedly. Though not poisonous, they can become very aggressive if confronted. They tend to mimic the rattlesnake by coiling, shaking its tail in the air vigorously, hissing loudly, and "striking" at its foe. Of course having no rattles and no fangs, it is all for show. Black racers, as they are known by many folk, have been known to give chase to a human interloper, making them all the more frightening.

For many years a family of black racers produced generations of their young in our woodpile near the cabin. It was not an unusual occurrence to see or even walk up on one or more of these sleek black reptiles. These harmless snakes serve a useful purpose as do all of Father Nature's creatures, catching vermin and driving away other snakes, particularly rattlers. Still, if someone comes upon one unexpectedly, it can strike fear in the heart of even the most stouthearted human because of its aggressiveness and mimicry of its cousin the rattlesnake.

One of our first confrontations with a timber rattler was the summer Kate's late mother visited us at the cabin. "Grammy", who was four feet eleven inches and weighed about 87 pounds, was fearless except for snakes and stinging insects. She had proved to be allergic to bees when she was but thirteen years old and had been terrified of them since. She was quite familiar with the story of the Garden of Eden, and hated (feared) snakes with a passion.

One day we took a walk along the old path to the original water supply. She was leading the way and suddenly walked up on a rattler coiled in the path directly in front of her. We expected her to panic and demand to be borne atop my shoulders post haste from the cabin to transportation back to her home in Georgia. But surprisingly, Grammy took the sighting of the snake with surprising calmness. She stopped abruptly, stood stock still, and stared at the timber rattler unmoving, until I removed the reptile from the path. After I tossed the snake into the bushes, we continued on our hike. I wouldn't have believed the circumstances of this encounter if I had not witnessed it in person. Probably aware of Grammy's fear of snakes, I believe that one of the green woodland imps created the occasion just to scare her. It didn't work, but I was sure that the gremlin had other tricks in its repertoire just waiting for a chance to cause mischief.

As a general practice, we do not bother snakes in the wild, but will destroy poisonous species when they venture into the cabin yard and pose a threat. Once, while doing woodwork and using a table set in front of my workshop, I turned to fetch something from inside the shop, and when I returned to the work table a timber rattler slithered out from under a low-lying shelf on the table. There's no doubt I had been standing within a foot of the snake for quite some time, possibly an hour or so. When my heart rate slowed to about 200, I escorted the reptile into the forest grateful that it had not seen fit to sink its fangs into my leg. Not once did the snake sound its warning rattles, even when I lifted it up on a stick for its aerial trip from the yard. It was about as friendly as any snake I've encountered, venomous or not.

I had a face to face encounter with another timber rattlesnake that was equally as startling to both the snake and me. Our cabin has a crawl space that houses the pipes, electrical wires, and the hot and cold water tanks. I venture into the cramped space to make repairs and to change the water filter attached to the mainline water intake. On this particular day, while hunched over in the limited space, I looked into the eyes of a timber rattler a few feet away. I had no idea how the snake found its way into the crawl space as I had put heavy screen wire over all the air vents. But there it was, and there I was, both frozen to our spots. I had no wriggle room; not even enough room to turn around without shifting closer to the invader. The rattler made no move to leave the crawl space. It lay calmly where I had first spotted it, not even sounding its rattles, just keeping a wary eye on me. I inched backwards as best I could. The snake watched with its "snake eyes", but made no move. Once out of the crawl space, I retrieved my shotgun and killed the intruder with one blast, managing to miss the entanglements of water pipes and electric lines. It turned out to be a very young snake with only two rattles and one button. Despite my fear during the confrontation, I couldn't help feeling a little remorse at slaying the docile reptile.

Our daughter and her friend Mary Lou DelFino were berry picking down the mountainside one summer day when they spied a snake in the bushes where they were working. Deb ran home to ask me to get rid of the snake. I took my shotgun and followed her back to the sighting of the snake. It turned out to be a timber rattler, so I shot the critter for the safety of the youngsters. Then the strangest thing happened; lo and behold the snake began to crawl off without its head! And backwards to boot! Now, I'd heard the old folk tale that a snake doesn't die until sundown, but this was ridiculous. I moved around the bushes and saw another timber rattler trying to slither away so I shot it too. Then I solved the mystery of the first snake moving without its head. The two snakes had been mating and were still conjugally attached. I really felt bad about dispatching the pair of snakes, especially during their procreation activities, but I had to put the girls' safety first.

Before the phoebes mentioned previously, decided on the upper eave of the cabin to build their nests, they tried a couple of other places. One year we arrived to find that they had constructed their nest on top of the electric light just outside of the kitchen door. We locked the kitchen door and steered clear of their nest as we waited for eggs to hatch and the chicks to fledge. A few days later, while lounging on the deck, but before the hatchlings were ready to fly away, we were astonished see an enormous blacksnake, completely ignoring us, attempting to climb up to the nest. We decided that absent anything on which the snake could gain traction the nestlings were safe. But we didn't reckon with the ingenuity of the reptile. As we watched, it seemed to assess the challenge for several minutes (was it communicating with the gremlin?). After a few minutes, it raised the upper part of its body about two feet, reminding us of the King Cobras we had seen in Africa, slipped its head through the door handle, and from there was able to find some footing (I use this term loosely). It could now cling to the upper door jamb and reach the nest.

At this point, we had seen enough. I grabbed its tail, pulled it down from the door and flung it over the side of the deck into the woods, all six feet of it! I don't know how mama phoebe felt, but the blacksnake was furious, hissing, spitting and otherwise demonstrating its desire to have another go at me. The adult phoebes, which had been perched nearby, fussing at the snake, now returned to the nest. We kept a wary eye out for the predator until the chicks had successfully flown the nest. We were pleased that we had foiled the dastardly gremlin's plans again, but what about next year?

When the nest was vacated, we moved it to a platform I constructed beneath the over-hang at the end of the deck. Kate and I felt sure that no snake could navigate the stone chimney and the cabin's aluminum siding to reach the new relocation. But one day, the following year, we saw a big black reptile already coiled around the nest. We didn't know if it was the same snake from our encounter a year earlier, but it was at least as large and just as aggressive. I carefully (fearfully?) grabbed the snake's tail and tugged, but unfortunately it did not relinquish its stranglehold on the nest and down came snake, nest, and chicks. The newly hatched birds were still alive when they hit the ground, but too immature to survive. Mama Phoebe was mad, the snake was mad, and we were mad. Was that the sniggering of the gremlin coming from a nearby tree?

We have found blacksnakes on our porch and even in our living room, but they are so fast and elusive that they disappear before we can take any action against them. I've searched diligently for their entranceways to no avail; finally concluding that our nemesis, the gremlin, is responsible for their appearances. Once, in the middle of the night, I stumbled on one in the living room just in front of Kate's reading chair. I switched on an overhead light to deal with the invader, but again it was too quick. It darted beneath the living room couch. I turned the couch over to try and catch the snake, but it was nowhere to be found. There was no hole it could have gone through to escape, at least one that I could find, but there was no other explanation for its escape. (Couldn't have been my imagination; no way!) From that time on, we always carry a flashlight with us if we wander around at night; either that or we turn on overhead lights which we are reluctant to do as it usually wakes the one of us still abed. I know that the blacksnakes are harmless and beneficial (they eat mice) but Kate and I can be a danger to ourselves trying to elude them should we happen on one while half asleep. I have never been able to find where they enter. Kate surprised another racer on the porch one morning. She screamed and the snake simply disappeared into thin air, no doubt the workings of our house gremlin (couldn't have been Kate's imagination; no way!)

    The only other snake we've seen near the cabin besides the timber rattler and the blacksnake are small corn snakes--usually no longer than a foot. We find their membranous skin more often that the snake itself; on the hearth, the indoor woodpile, and on the screen window sill.

These little snakes like to hide on top of the part of the deck pillars not covered by joists. I suppose they lie there waiting for a stray mouse to come by.

Once in a while, we'll find a tiny ring-neck snake either in the cabin or under the deck. The cute little reptiles are hardly bigger than earthworms, shiny black skin with a bright yellow ring around their neck. Against Mother Nature's rules, I sometimes play with the little snakes before moving them away from the cabin. One year, I saw a coachwhip crossing the yard. They slither along with their head raised a few inches above the ground. The long skinny reptiles are interesting to watch, but somehow seem a little sinister, maybe because they remind us of the way we've seen cobras move about in Africa and Asia.

Our nearest neighbors down the mountain discovered a copperhead snake's lair under a large boulder near their house, and over the years they have had dozens of these venomous reptiles show up in their yard. One year, their dog evidently stuck its nose into the snakes den, as he showed up back at the house with his head swollen the size of a watermelon. We happened to visit during the time of the dog's recovery. It was a pitiable sight to say the least. We are thankful that we've never seen a copperhead on our property. These snakes are smaller but more aggressive than the timber rattlers.

Deer are so common that they deserve scant mention. They appear in our yard, drink from Kate's oasis and they even eat certain vegetation we try to care for. Once we planted 100 pine trees that were donated to us by the Arboretum Conservancy; the deer ate all of them! Not very long after taking possession of the cabin, our dog Bleau, raised a doe and fawn nearby and gave chase. The doe took off through the woods lickety-split, while the fawn followed its instincts and froze in a thicket. When I was finally able to corral Bleau, I returned to the scene to check on the fawn which turned out to be only a couple of weeks old. I lifted the tiny deer and took it to the cabin for Kate to see. The fawn looked amazingly like our dog, light beige in color, slender with long legs, and big eyes. Kate was napping and when I roused her, carrying the fawn in my arms, she immediately thought I was carrying Bleau and that something really dreadful had happened to our pet. Humans should not interfere with nature. I know I broke a rule of nature when I brought the fawn for Kate to see, so I quickly returned the fawn to the exact spot where I had found it. All the time I held the little deer, even when I placed it back where I had found it, the tiny creature never moved or made a sound. No sooner had I walked away from the thicket, mama doe returned and led her offspring down the mountainside, both apparently none the worse for the incident.

That's not the only role Bleau has played. Many years ago, we were owned by a yellow tabby cat named "Buttercup", or "Busty" for short. Busty was a very docile and loving cat and didn't like to be separated from his minions. One day, Kate, Deb, and I decided to hike up the mountain. We had forgotten that Busty was lazing on the deck. When he missed us, he ambled up the trail behind us. We noticed him following us only after we had walked quite some distance. Just as we spotted Busty, Bleau roused a deer and gave chase. Frightened, Busty hid in some bushes. After rounding up Bleau, we searched for Busty so we could take him back to the cabin and lock him inside. But Busty was nowhere to be found. We combed the area where we last saw him, but no cat. Finally, as we were about to give up hoping the cat would find its way home; Deb spotted the furry yellow ball hiding in some debris beneath some bushes. He had followed his instincts like the fawn had done and froze under cover.

Bleau was a very territorial dog and was totally fearless, all 20 pounds of skin and bones, which is usual for the Whippet breed. Our closet neighbors walked up one Sunday and allowed their dog, a full-grown German shepherd, to follow them. As soon as their dog appeared, Bleau attacked. She was a 20-pound bundle of ferociousness. The larger dog tolerated her antagonist for a couple of minutes before snapping a two inch tear in Bleau's shoulder. The wound was too serious for us to treat, so we had to take her to the vet. The lesion healed, but the flap of skin never grew fur again. As an aside, Bleau was a pedigree whippet whose mother was a past grand champion of the breed. Such a scar would have disqualified her as a show dog, but she was born with a bent tail so she didn't measure up to the kennel standards anyway. In fact, the bent tail and a heart murmur amplified our affection for the little whippet. We kept Bleau, bent tail, scar, and heart murmur for over a dozen years. She died by our side when we lived in South Africa.

Of all the animals on the mountain with which we have been friend or foe, the most exciting (sometime more excitement that we wanted!) and interesting have been the black bears. When we bought the property, Mr. Larrick told us that many years before black bears were plentiful on the mountain, but that in recent years hunting and encroachment on their territory had driven them away. It was a rare occasion to see any of these creatures on Great North Mountain; indeed, we never saw a bear during the first twenty-five years visiting our cabin. It seems that the black bear population has outgrown its usual habitat in George Washington National Park, and they have gradually returned to Great North Mountain.

The first time we saw a bear on our property was about six years ago. Kate was sleeping in that morning. I was lounging on the deck. I heard a noise that I knew wasn't a bird in the underbrush that borders our clearing. I focused my attention there and was stunned to see a rather large brown bear; black bears come in different hues, this black bear was brown. I've seen bears from time to time during our tent-camping days, but to see one on our property for the first time in over 20 years, caused my heart to implant itself in my throat. I croaked a call to rouse Kate so she could see this phenomenon. She didn't respond, probably because she thought she heard a bull frog. So I hurried back to the bedroom and rousted her. We watched the bruin from our bedroom window saunter across out yard into the woods behind the cabin. I'm no bear expert, but he looked to be rather old and weigh somewhere between 200 and 300 pounds. We were quite excited to see our first bear on Great North Mountain. It was not to be the last time. After that sighting, we began to see the occasional bears, usually at some distance, crossing from one ravine to the other. We've spotted several territorial markings made by a bear stretching up to its highest and scratching its mark on a tree trunk. But, several experiences in particular stand in our memories.

One evening, we heard a commotion near my workshop where we keep a garbage barrel for use when the inside container is full and we aren't ready for a trip down the mountain to the Gore city dump. At first we thought that the gremlins were at work again, everyone knows they go bump in the night. But after consideration, we surmised that it was probably the devilish little masked denizens, also known as raccoons. Arming myself with a one million watt flashlight, I crept out into the darkness. Cautiously, I peeked around our parked SUV, shined the light on the garbage barrel. Nothing. Then I glanced toward my shop door and looked straight into the eyes of a prowling black bear standing about six feet away and gazing quizzically at me. The monster looked to weigh 600 pounds through my saucer-sized eyes, but it was probably less than half that weight.

My muscles went rigid! It was as if I had turned into a pillar of granite. I couldn't move for all of five seconds that felt like minutes. When I regained some mobility, I flashed the light into the bear's eyes temporarily blinding it and slowly backed away until I could safely duck into the cabin. The bear, obviously not perturbed in the least by our encounter, went back to exploring my shop area. Kate and I went to the back door of the porch and made a racket to scare the bear away; they are supposed to run when humans make loud noises. This bruiser simply looked our direction with a quizzical stare and continued its exploration. Well when that didn't work, I retrieved my shotgun and fired some buckshot into the trees above the bruin's head causing leaves, twigs and pellets to rain down on the interloper. That caught its attention and he or she scampered off into the woods none the worse for the episode.

I often get up before Kate and make coffee, read the news on my computer, and station myself on the deck to await her to join me bird-watching. I also use this quiet time to read any current event magazine I happen to have. This particular morning, I was engrossed reading the latest issue of U. S. News and World Report reporting on the strife around the world. An unusual noise caught my attention. Our in-house gremlin makes noises often, mostly at night, so I wasn't concerned about this one. It sounded a little like the clicking of a cricket. I lowered the magazine and casually turned toward the sound. Nope, it wasn't the gremlin; it was a huge male black bear! As it rounded the corner from the walkway by the kitchen his claws were causing the clicking sound as they struck the wood planking of the deck. I was stricken with the frog-in-throat syndrome again for several seconds.

Allowing for my startled condition, I estimated this boar's weight to be well above 300lbs. He stopped ten feet away and stared. After regaining my senses, I stood on the settee I had been sitting on, waved my magazine and croaked unintelligible sounds. According to what I had read, this was supposed to frighten black bears away. The bear turned around slowly, retraced its steps down the deck past the kitchen and into the yard. It didn't seem at all frightened, just annoyed. As soon as the frog in my windpipe allowed me to make sounds humans could understand I called Kate to see what I had found. We watched the bear disappear into the woods.

Kate doesn't always sleep later than I. On one occasion, she rose earlier than usual and strolled out onto the deck, still half asleep, to welcome the new day on the mountain. I was still performing my ablutions in the bathroom when I heard her shout, "Come see what I've found!" She had "found" a bear asleep beneath the folding chaise lounge. Her shout woke the medium-sized bruin who lurched to its feet, noisily casting aside the aluminum lounge. Amid the clashing of the chaise lounge, Kate's shouting, and my stumbling through the cabin, the bruin vacated its erstwhile slumber pad and dashed posthaste off the deck and into the woods

Another time, Kate "found" a full-grown bear resting against the porch screen door fast asleep. The bear had evidently not tried to enter, but simply decided to take a nap and the screen door offered a good back rest. The napping bear looked much like the first one we saw crossing the cabin clearing. It was a male, brown, large, and appeared to be quite old. He roused himself slowly and ambled off into the forest when we made a commotion.

One year we had our mountain SUV in Florida for some reason, so when we returned to the cabin, we had to drive two vehicles. Kate drove our sedan to Atlanta for a visit with our offspring while I drove the SUV straight to the mountain. I arrived several days before she did.

I went to town for some groceries and returned to the cabin at dusk, and since I had not left any lights on the visibility was limited. When I stepped onto the walkway to the kitchen door, a massive dark form loomed before me. A bear had been loitering on the deck, for what reason I have no idea. I froze, it froze. The bear moved toward me, but I quickly deduced that the startled animal wanted to return to the forest and I was in its way. I quickly moved out of the bear's escape route. It just as quickly lumbered past me, but stopped at the edge of the clearing as if to cogitate on what had just transpired, and to see what I had in mind. I quickly demonstrated that I wasn't interested in another tete-a-tete by going inside and closing the wood door. The big fellow stood for about three or four minutes staring at the door, and then melted into the darkness.

Another time I arose at my usual time and plopped myself on the deck settee to watch for new varieties of birds. I casually surveyed the clearing as usual when it seemed at first that one of the boulders in front of the deck moved. Then a couple of the smaller rocks ones followed suit. It took a few seconds for my sleepy brain and eyes to understand that boulders and rocks don't move by themselves, and besides they aren't usually black. A sow and her two cubs rose, sleepily surveyed the clearing just as I had, and then headed down the ravine toward the stream.

Our granddaughter, Michelle, a high school All-American soccer player, was visiting and seeking a bit of level landscape to practice when she stopped dead in her tracks as a large bear (all woodland bears are large when one stumbles on them unexpectedly) sauntered out of the woods directly in her path. After glancing at the soccer ball and deciding he or she was not interested in a one on one soccer dust up, the bear, with a side glance, continued meandering down the mountainside. The bear probably thought the petrified young girl soccer player standing immobile nearby was made of alabaster anyway, and therefore nothing to be concerned with.

Once the black bears began to move back to Great North Mountain, they routinely upended bird feeders, ate the contents, and sometimes destroyed the feeder as well. As previously recounted, I began to string the feeders high enough the bears couldn't reach them, but that didn't stop them or the raccoons from trying. Kate and I had started getting up during the night once in a while to shoo the animals away or sometimes just to watch their antics while trying to reach the bird seed. The in-house gremlin helps with these matters as it often makes some kind of noise to disturb our sleep. On one of these nightly sojourns, I grabbed my powerful flashlight and went onto the deck. When I got out of bed, Kate looked at the bedside clock; it was 4:30 a.m. I flashed the light on the "gazebo" feeder hanging over the path to the spring from which we get our drinking water.

There, just below the feeder a black bear sow was stretching upward toward the feeder. The light frightened her and she bounded into the brush. I called Kate to see the bear. When she arrived on the deck, she spotted both the sow and at least one cub crashing through the forest. We estimated the small cub to probably be about three or four months old, certainly less than a year.

The most recent encounter with a mountain bear occurred during the middle of one night. Kate and I were awakened by a strange, rather loud noise that sounded as if was on the cabin deck. At first, I attributed the racket to our gremlin that often makes noises during the night. But this was different. Both Kate and I arose, grabbed a flashlight we keep just under the side of the bed and crept toward the doors leading to the deck. We looked out but saw nothing unusual that would account for the noise, so we returned to bed. Next morning as I entered the kitchen to make our morning coffee, the cause of the commotion from the previous night was self-evident. The screen over the kitchen sink was pushed inward, shredded and lying in the basin.

All evidence pointed to a bear attempting to enter the kitchen, probably drawn by residual kitchen odors. Apparently we had frightened the beast away when we stumbled into the area with flashlights beaming. Had the uninvited guest actually got into the house, the situation could have become dicey as it would have been hard for the intruder to clamber over the kitchen sink and leave by the same way it had entered. All the other exits were blocked by locked doors. The whole episode was probably quite exciting for both us humans and for the bear, but not as exciting as it would have been had we cornered the bruin in our kitchen. I repaired the screen the same day and hoped the misguided bruin would not return.

Most of the wildlife we come in contact with is avian. The songbirds are a delight for Kate who has been cataloging her sightings since recuperating from a surgery when we lived in New York. I bought a chaise lounge and a pair of good binoculars that she used every day during her convalescence to watch the numerous varieties of birds that visited our wooded backyard.

Among the many species we see, perhaps the most cunning are wild turkeys as any turkey hunter will attest. We don't see them often, but sometimes we see them in large flocks of a dozen or more. Once, to the utter delight of Kate's aged father, we came upon a flock of over two dozen birds. These magnificent birds are the wiliest of the fowl.

The turkey was once proposed by Benjamin Franklin to be our national bird because of its cunning and regal appearance. I wonder why the sobriquet came to refer to silly acts by humans.

Other species we see during our summer stays include: goldfinch, titmouse, chickadee, nuthatch, and several varieties of woodpeckers. Each year Kate hangs feeders containing sugar water. Soon thereafter, hummingbirds visit, sometimes in flocks, sometimes one or two. We get a lot of enjoyment watching these tiny little feathered balls with two-inch beaks suck up the sweet water Kate puts out for them.

Usually during the summer, Kate will spot and identify others less plentiful, indeed some rare migrating species. One of the more pleasant pastimes is to take a lunch down to the little stream flowing from our cistern and watch the several species visit for a bath and preening. We watch the same practice at Kate's "oasis" from the comfort of the cabin porch. Keeping the feeders supplied is a daily job, often requiring repairs resulting from nightly visits from bears, raccoons, opossums and flying squirrels.

According to our books on wild animals and their ranges, porcupines do not inhabit Great North Mountain, but our neighbors had a difficult time convincing their German shepherd of that when she came home from the woods with a dozen or so quills embedded in her snout. Difficult indeed! We've never had such a "lucky" encounter. The same sources assure us that there are no mountain lions in Shenandoah Mountains where we live. Yet, there have been reported sightings of a large beige colored cat, presumably a mountain lion on Great North Mountain.

One day as we were starting on a hike, following an old road we no longer use, we found several bones that were obviously from a full-grown deer. Part of the hide and many of the bones were missing, so out of curiosity, I climbed up the embankment that ran alongside the road and discovered scraps of a carcass and the missing bones six feet above those on the old road.

Though it's not unheard of, bears usually do not consider a full-grown deer as normal prey, although bears being omnivorous beasts, might feast on a carcass they stumble onto. Unless a bear came upon a dead deer and dragged the animal up the bank, which I consider illogical, my guess is that a mountain lion killed the deer. Teeth marks found on the bones lent more to the theory that it was a cat rather than a bear. A bear would probably have crushed the bones for marrow. No other animal on the mountain would have been strong enough to carry a deer kill up the steep bank. Besides, we learned while in Africa that dragging a fresh kill high enough to thwart the efforts of pesky scavengers is routine for the large cats.

We've never seen any other signs that could be ascribed to a mountain lion, but the strange sounds we occasionally hear keep us leaning in favor of a big cat that lives somewhere on Great North Mountain, perhaps in the caves on top of the mountain. One of our neighbors has reportedly seen such an animal several times while driving home from her job. She's lived on the mountain for more than 30 years, so we are reluctant to question her claims. We have occasionally heard noises during the night that sound like the screaming of panthers that I remember hearing on camping trips in Florida when I was a boy. The grottos I've mentioned before that are scattered among the boulders along the Appalachian Trail are ideally suited to mountain lion lairs.

Kate and I have heard coyotes howling once in a while and others on the mountain have seen the wary animals. We are not surprised that the wily critters inhabit the mountain as they have proliferated throughout the eastern states, even in cities. We don't question the claims of other mountain folk that these canines are with us.

We've spotted the sly foxes on a few occasions and sadly often find their remains on the roads in and out of the mountains. And our neighbor living at the foot of the mountain will readily testify to their existence, as they have proof of "a fox in the henhouse" (to borrow an old maxim). They keep a flock of chickens. Their chickens are consistently preyed upon by foxes, weasels, raccoons and perhaps coyotes as well.

Before deciding that it was a bad idea, other neighbors used to entice the foxes up to their house by leaving kitchen refuse out. Kate and I watched a family appear there when we were visiting the neighbors. Very entertaining, but we all decided that it's best not to fool with Father Nature, so they stopped the practice.

A few years ago a colony of flying squirrels took up residence near us and visited our bird feeders. At times as many as eight have performed their acrobatics, a fascinating show to watch, in the trees near the cabin deck as they enjoyed feasting on a special blend of bird food containing dried fruit and peanuts, bought especially for them. They became so accustomed to us sitting on the deck watching their playful antics that had we wished to do so, we could have touched them. Our granddaughter Michelle, did in fact pet one once.

One year, they nested in an owl house I had constructed in hopes of luring up some screech owls. Once we discovered them, we could tap on the wood owl box and watch as one or more heads of the loveable little squirrels would pop up to see what was going on. Their tiny heads with huge eyes reminded us a lot of the "bush babies" (also known as night apes, or nacht apies in Afrikaans) that we searched for during night safaris in Africa.

Unfortunately, the tiny flying acrobats began to chew on the wood paneling of the cabin porch. We couldn't determine if they were eating the paint or using the wood fiber for nest material. Their gnawing created an annoying sound and left an unsightly aftermath though not structurally damaging. We had to continually spot paint the raw wood after the outside layer was stripped off. The squirrels all but disappeared about two years ago; we only see one or two occasionally nowadays. We hope that their gnawing the painted paneling and their disappearance is not connected. We still put out food that they like and some nights one or two will pay us a visit. They don't gnaw on the porch panels anymore. That's good, but we don't know why they don't.

Timothy Veach, a son of our neighbor, came upon a wounded Great Horned Owl, rehabilitated it, and released the huge bird into the forest near the cabin. The disappearance of the flying squirrels coincided with the release, perhaps coincidentally, but we also don't see as many chipmunks either. Kate places an ear of corn on a specially built feeder each morning and sometimes one or two chipmunks will come up on the deck to feed, but before the owl showed up, we'd see several competing for the corn. There seems to be a reduction of bird sightings as well since the owl took up residence in the woods near the cabin.

The owl is tolerant of humans, probably because of its rehabilitation, and we often see it perched on a tree limb near the cabin. Once while sitting on the deck at dusk, the big bird swooped down for a flying squirrel on a tree branch no more than five or six feet in front of us. Fortunately for the squirrel, it was able to avoid the attack and survived. Brant and Kevin spied the owl capturing a snake in the clearing behind the cabin. I guess, on balance, Kate and I are happy to have the big fellow around.

Anyone having spent any time in the forest knows that there are certain things with which one must contend. Bugs in the woods are a natural phenomenon; they include ticks, chiggers, ants and all sorts of flying insects. Most of these pests can be warded off with some repellent. Others cannot be avoided; they just come with the territory, so to speak. The woods are abundant with small thumb sized woodland mice that seem to find a way into the cabin no matter what is done to keep them at bay. While we are away during the winter, the little rascals sometimes invade cozy places inside the cabin where they make their nests during the cold months. Routinely, Kate and I must check the likely places and clean up after them. The most exasperating choice of the mice is my vehicle that I leave up on the mountain during the winter months. They have on occasion built nests inside the headliner, in the air ducts and behind the dash. I once had a Mazda truck that the mice claimed as their very own. When I traded the truck in on another vehicle, I was embarrassed to present the truck cum mice haven. The smell from their excretions was really raunchy. I was surprised that the car dealer did not require a payment from me to take the infested vehicle off my hands.

I tried mothballs in our vehicles for a couple of winters. The mice did avoid close proximity to the odiferous little white balls, but passengers wanted to do the same. People riding in the vehicle strewn with mothballs carried the odor with them after alighting from the vehicle. I heard or read somewhere that mice would avoid Bounce dryer sheets, but doubted the authenticity of the information. However, one fall on departing the mountain, I stashed the dryer sheets all around the vehicle we left behind. Next spring, there wasn't a sign of the pesky, though cute, little pests. In subsequent years, we have had like success with this procedure. I've even spread them around my shop which had been a haven for the mice in past years. When I tried another brand of dryer sheets they did not provide the same success. The dryer sheets must be Bounce; generic brands do not work as well. Nobody complains about the pleasant odor as they did with the stench of mouse urine and the stench of the acrid odor of mothballs. We followed the same procedure for the likely nesting places of the mice in the cabin. Bounce did the job inside as well. We owe the magazine Good House Keeping for this hint.

Several years ago, we found a small Eastern Brown Bat roosting beneath the eave just outside the kitchen window. It was cute in an ugly sort of way. When we tapped lightly on the paneling below its roosting place, it would open an eye for a few seconds and then ignore us. At night we could see the little bat zooming back and forth in front of the cabin where bugs tended to gather when there was a light on. We named the little hairy flying rodent Homer; why? No particular reason. Every summer on arrival, we looked for the bat in its usual place. Some years it did not appear for several weeks, but eventually returned to its special place under the eave. But two years ago it failed to show up and we've not seen it since. We read that bats, particularly this specie, have been attacked by what the biologist called "white nose fungus". We assumed that our little visitor succumbed to that ailment. We still miss seeing the little furry ball hanging upside down under the eave. We probably have more bugs at night too.

Some readers will no doubt cringe at our confrontations with potentially dangerous animals or think us overly sentimental at our attachment to others, such as the little Eastern Brown bat, but these associations are an integral part of our refuge on Great North Mountain.

Chapter IV: Mountain Flora

Great North Mountain supports a plethora of plants and trees for nature lovers. The most plentiful trees are chestnut oak, so named because the leaves resemble those of the chestnut. Father Nature has also provided: hickories, tulip poplars, sour gum, birch, locust, Virginia pine and others.

Unfortunately the once plentiful chestnut trees have been devastated by a foreign beetle that encircles the trunk killing the tree from that point upward. The roots remain alive and struggle continually to send out shoots only to have them face the same fate as the mature trees. Only those chestnuts in protected areas remain alive.

Thousands of these majestic and highly useful trees were killed thirty or so years ago in the Great Smokey Mountains. Today, gazing from Clingman's Dome, the highest point in the park, the destruction caused by the relentless little beetle is evident as far as the eye can see. Luckily Great North Mountain has an abundance of other species to compensate for the beetle's destruction.

The whole family has enjoyed the shady canopies of the dogwood trees in the cabin clearing during the hot summer months. Kate and I have often sat in the shade beneath the spreading branches to watch for birds, or simply to enjoy the tranquility of the forest. Many people know the beauty of the domesticated pink dogwoods that have been planted all around the country. Unlike the domesticated varieties, the wild dogwoods have only white blossoms, they are nonetheless beautiful trees in all seasons with bright red berries in the fall and winter. The birds feast on the berries that almost look like small cherries.

Regrettably, the flowering dogwood trees, both wild and hybrid, have been attacked, we are told by the county agent, by a disease akin to the anthrax that attacks bovines. Several of these elegant trees near the cabin are infected and some have died. Others continue to wage a losing battle, sadly dying limb by limb. Perhaps we could save them if we lived at the cabin year round and could apply an antidote on a regular basis. Hybrid dogwoods (pink blossoms) planted as ornamentals survive when they are cared for.

The stately hickory and oak trees have begun to suffer from some malady as well. We have watched more than a dozen of these fine trees slowly die from some kind of disease. And more is the pity we can't do anything about it. The problem started when we had a heavy infestation of gypsy moths about five years ago. The pests particularly favored the hickory and chestnut oaks. Those trees the gypsy moth larvae did not kill outright were left in a weakened state and have slowly succumbed to other diseases. The Virginia State Department of Forestry sprayed the gypsy moth infested areas, which included that of our cabin. One year before they sprayed, sitting on our deck we could hear the eerie sound of the thousands of droppings as the worms devoured the leaves of the surrounding trees. It was a sad and repulsive experience. Sprayings have controlled the damage from the voracious larvae, but the old adage, for every action there is often unintentional consequences, has played out in this case. We have noticed with deep regret the reduction of the bird population since the treatments began. We hoped the sprayings would drive off the forest gremlins as well, but no such luck.

One of Kate's favorite trees is the Juneberry or serviceberry. As an avid birdwatcher she knows that the tree's berries are cherished by many songbirds, some that come only when the bright red berries are present in the spring and disappear until the ensuing year. Mountain laurel, sassafras, allspice, blueberry, raspberry, blackberry, maypops, chicory, and a host of others cover the forest floor. Nothing rivals the splendor of the mountainside on Great North Mountain when resplendent with flowering mountain laurel. The height of the blooming season occurs before we arrive at the cabin each summer, but we enjoy the end of Mother Nature's splendiferous show.

We eat all the blueberries we can collect before the bears and other animals get to them first. The tiny wild blueberries are a particular delight as their taste far outshines the larger domestic varieties. These plants too, have dwindled over the last few years causing a mad scramble to beat the animals to fruit of the fewer remaining bushes.

The early settlers made good use of nearly all the wild plants. They used the leaves and berries of the very pleasant smelling allspice bush to make their own all-purpose spice, chicory roots to supplement scarce coffee, the leaves and roots of sassafras for tea, drunk as remedies for certain ailments as well as just for the pleasant aroma and taste, and the yellow lemony flavored maypop fruit for jams and jellies. Oddly, every part of the maypop plant, a member of the mandrake family, is toxic, except the fruit. This perhaps makes the fruit psychologically more appealing. We think that the mountain nymphs thrive on the plants; they are apparently immune to the poisonous leaves.

Kate and I have tried several of the pioneer recipes using the plants listed above. However, like most folks we find it's usually easier to buy the ingredients off the grocer's shelf than scavenging the forest. Still, we brew a cup of sassafras tea from time to time from the leaves we can gather easily.

We found that chewing on a sweet cherry-birch twig or a succulent sassafras stem while hiking through the woods is a pleasant treat. History says Shawnee Indians did likewise to quench their thirst as they trotted over the mountain to raid the white settlements on the other side. It's okay to chew the stem of the wild cherry as well, but most people don't because of the slight cyanic taste. The berries from this tree are not tasty for the same reason, but settlers used them to ferment their wine. Birch beer was once made from the sap of the plentiful Cherry Birch trees, but the harvesting gave way to artificial flavoring. The resulting drink is usually called "root beer" nowadays.

When the cabin was built, we cut only the trees absolutely necessary for the small cabin clearing. We like the nearness of the trees, the privacy they afford, the soughing of the breeze through the branches, the shelter they provide for the birds, and the cooling power in hot summer months. We have bonded with the trees as we have the wild birds and mourn the death of either. Sometimes we hear a tree falling in the woods near us. It is scary at times until we know it isn't one that is close enough to fall on us, and then we feel saddened at the loss of another of these majestic plants.

When the cabin septic system was installed, we had to clear a space for the drain field. When the installation was finished, we noticed a small tulip poplar sapling remaining on the edge of the drain field. It was about three feet tall and far enough from the cabin wall as not to be a problem. We both admired the fully grown trees and their tulip-like blossoms from which their common name is derived scattered about in the woods so we left the sapling. Thirty-eight years later, the sprout we saved has grown to over 100 feet tall and has an almost perfect shape. Each year it is loaded with tulip blossoms. Kate and I often sit on a bench we installed nearby to watch for birds and admire the tulip tree while complementing ourselves for having the good sense to leave it when all the other nearby trees had to be pushed down. It was a serendipitous decision indeed. Later, when we added the screen porch, we had to draw up plans that would accommodate the beautiful giant.

Though we could reap a tidy sum if we allowed the hardwood trees on our property to be lumbered, we so thoroughly detest the condition of the forest left by commercial timber harvesting that we have never considered allowing the trees to be cut. We recognize the continuing economic need for lumber, and know that, like other renewable resources, selective harvesting of the trees could be done, but we have no intention of ever cutting any live trees from our refuge, selective or otherwise. The only trees we take down are dead ones we can use for firewood.

Chapter V: Gremlins

Throughout this narrative, Kate and I have referred to gremlins, nymphs, imps, woodland spirits, etc. With our tongues planted firmly in our cheeks, we continue to blame these imps when things go wrong with no apparently logical reason. Besides, who are we to say trolls don't exist in Norway, waldgeist in Germany, and gremlins in the WWII airplanes of the British and American Air Force? Or, that the Yeti in the Alps, Bigfoot in Louisiana bayous, or Sasquatch in the north woods of Oregon and Washington don't exist? What we do know is that there are many inexplicable events that occur on Great North Mountain. Waldgeist? Who knows? In the following narrative, we recount some of these happenings with just a trace of farcical humor.

When we lived in New Jersey, we sometimes visited the cabin during the late fall and early winter months when the weather forecast was favorable. One year, Deb invited one of her girlfriends to join us for the Thanksgiving holiday. The forecast was for a beautiful weekend with trees wearing their straggling fall colors, and moderate temperatures prevailing. There was no mention of snow or freezing conditions. As we slept on that Thanksgiving night, a bank of snow clouds wafted quietly over the mountain and clothed Great North Mountain in a blanket of soft glistening snow over a foot deep. When we awoke, we were astonished— nothing like this ever happens in November! What kind of magical nymph would manage such a feat? The forest was a sparkling wonderland! The sun was shining and the air was clear and cold. We could see a few deer in the distance pawing in the snow for grass and with a cloud of mist rising with each breath. But otherwise the woods were silent, enveloped in an awesome quietness.

Then the gremlin, nonplussed at our lack of concern, caused the temperature to drop steadily into the teens as the day wore on, and by sunset, the top layer of snow that had melted in the sunlight, turned into a gleaming crust of ice. After several hours drinking in the stunning beauty of nature, it dawned on us that we were stranded. That's when the gremlin began to smile. All evidence of man's intervention into nature had been covered over, except for the upper portions of the electricity poles. Only the tops of bushes and small trees remained visible. The car we came up in was locked in an icy snowdrift higher than the wheels. As the evening progressed, the weather outlook became bleaker. More snow began to fall and it became bitterly cold. We had no means of communication as our phone lines had not been installed and cellular phones had not become available. Now the gremlin was ecstatic.

We were in no danger; we had plenty of food and with ample fuel for our chain saw, firewood was available from nearby standing dead trees, so we simply enjoyed the splendor of the scenery surrounding us and awaited a thaw we were sure would come in a few days. But we didn't count on the gremlin's determination. As the days passed with no indication that the thaw would come soon, the girls began to develop cabin fever, and besides they needed to get back to school as the Thanksgiving holidays were over. We discussed our options and finally agreed that the girls and I would hike off the mountain and try to arrange some way for them to return to New Jersey.

The three of us bundled up in winter garb and set out down the mountainside. We slogged all the way to Back Creek road where I flagged a retired forest ranger in his 4-wheel vehicle who luckily was on his way to Winchester. He agreed to take us to town and to give me a ride back on his return trip to his cabin on the mountain. In town, I arranged passage for the girls on a Greyhound bus and telephoned the parents of Deb's friend to meet them in New Jersey. Before leaving town, I notified my office that I was stranded on the mountain and would return to work as soon as I could free myself from our snowbound cabin. As promised, the retired ranger gave me a ride back to the bottom of Great North Mountain.

The Good Samaritan took me as far up the mountain as his vehicle could maneuver. He refused payment, so I thanked him profusely and began my grueling trek up the mountainside to the cabin. With each step, I crashed knee deep through the icy crust that had formed overnight. Walking on this configuration was a nightmare. The thin crust of ice could not bear my weight, and as I sank up to my thighs there was the danger of stepping on a hidden rock or fallen tree trunk that could easily cause a twisted ankle or knee. Anyone who has attempted to take the next step while the one leg is buried in a hole up to the thigh can appreciate my exhaustive climb. When I finally arrived back at the cabin and was warmed by a roaring fire, I was a tired miserable wreck.

The snowing stopped, but the bitter cold did not let up. About a week later, our food was running low and we had to forage farther and farther for firewood. We also developed a touch of cabin fever after being captives of the beautiful, but obdurate icy snow. We had no way of knowing how long the present conditions would last, so we drew up a plan to evacuate our little cabin and return to civilization.

First, we had to free up the car which the gremlin had mired. We hacked off the ice from around the wheels with an axe so I could install the heavy-duty tire chains we had purchased months before, and then we scraped a peephole in the frost covering the windshield. After winterizing the cabin, we coaxed the engine to life, and maneuvered the 5,000 lb. sedan to a clearing where we could see a clear pathway through the trees to the roadbed several hundred yards below. I cautioned Kate to hang on, but it was unnecessary as her hands were already clamped on the armrest in a frozen (pardon the pun) grip. We thumbed our noses at the gremlin, took a deep breath, eased the big Buick Electra into low gear, and literally snowboarded down the mountainside, somehow managing to dodge trees and stumps along the way with the chains providing a modicum of steerage. I don't think we breathed again during the whole time we were slipping and sliding down the mountain. To this day we can't remember a wilder ride; we still get goose bumps thinking about it. Notwithstanding our trials and tribulations, we still had a great Thanksgiving holiday with a roast turkey and all the trimmings. It was the most memorable Thanksgiving holiday we ever endured!

****

When my job took me to Japan on assignment, Kate and Deb accompanied me; Brant was attending Florida Southern College. After a year in Japan, we moved to Hong Kong. While away, we left the care of the cabin to our good friends, Wilton and Cookie Smith. For their use, they agreed to pay insurance and keep the place in good order. They encountered many of the gremlin's work as we had over the years; frozen pipes, leaking joints, invasive animals, and all the other tricks the gremlin could conjure up.

After our return, sadly, Wilton developed terminal cancer, but as his time was running out he and Cookie came to spend some time with us while we were at the cabin. Wilton and I sat on the deck recalling all the skirmishes with the gremlin we had endured and laughed like a couple of people without a care in the world. I am pleased and grateful that Wilton was able to enjoy a brief respite with me from his constant anxiety over his deteriorating health.

In February of 1979, my IBM tour in Hong Kong had come to an end; Kate and I were returning home; Deb had graduated from the Hong Kong International School and was matriculating at Vanderbilt University. Kate and I decided to take advantage of the hiatus between my assignments for a holiday in Hawaii. We booked into an upscale hotel in Maui, but the weather was unfit for a proper Hawaiian holiday. We wondered if the gremlin had met us on our USA return. It was rainy and cool and the hotel was expensive, so we left early. On the flight from Hawaii, we decided to spend the remaining time before starting my new assignment in New York at our cabin on Great North Mountain. We had been away for three years, living in some of the most densely populated places in the world, and looked forward to a pleasant return to nature. We rented a car at Dulles airport and headed for the mountain some 60 miles away. The weather had turned really cold, but seemingly even colder to us, as we had spent the last two years in a semi-tropical Hong Kong; no doubt our blood had become thinner.

After stopping by for enough groceries to last us for a week or so, we loaded the rental car, and drove to the bottom of the mountain. We were apprehensive of our decision as soon as we began to see patches of snow on the main roads leading from Winchester. We knew that the rental car had neither snow tires nor chains. We kept our hopes up, but when we turned onto Sawlog Road and started the gradual climb up the first incline, the tires lost purchase and the car slid to the side of the road. That was it. The rental car wasn't going any higher up the mountain. Now what?

We had long since forgotten about the mountain spirits and how they could foil almost any human endeavor in their domain. We stood cold and helpless beside the rental car. As with the vehicle, we were not equipped for cold weather. We glared angrily at the useless rental car, cursing the forces that put us into this situation. We had several bags of groceries in the back seat of the useless vehicle, and the cabin was at least a mile up the snow covered mountain. It was obvious to us that hiking to the cabin carrying the groceries from where we stood was out of the question.

Just as we had made up our minds to turn around and return to the comfort of a motel, our luck changed. The same retired forest ranger that had helped us before, came by in his 4-wheel drive Jeep and agreed to take us as close to the cabin as he could navigate. We transferred the several bags of groceries to his vehicle, while he looked on quizzically. We could imagine that he was thinking we were a couple of real dummies; only morons would put themselves in the predicament he found us. He took us to the foot of a hill that sloped steeply upward to the cabin, the highest level the ranger's vehicle could climb; the same place he had dropped me off once before. Kate and I off-loaded the bags and thanked him. He agreed to meet us in a week for the return trip to the rental car.

As the ranger drove away slowly shaking his head, we stared at the cabin and joined his headshaking. We silently agreed with the ranger's probable opinion of our lack of common sense, but having come this far, we were determined to make the best of a flawed venture. I particularly had great trepidation as I could vividly remember the trouble I had climbing this slope after taking Deb and her friend to town months before. And at that time I wasn't carrying anything.

We hugged two grocery sacks apiece and began struggling up the remaining incline. That trek proved to be excruciatingly slow and distressing, especially for Kate. Her shorter legs made her struggles more exasperating and tiring.

The freezing and thawing once again had caused alternate layers of snow and ice on the mountainside. Periodically we would break through the ice on the surface and crash knee deep into the second layer causing us to spill our groceries. After retrieving the spilled food and replacing it in the now soggy paper sacks, we'd extract our legs and take another few steps, stop, rest, gaze upwards at the cabin, and then plod another yard or two. It didn't seem to get any closer. Was it a mirage concocted by the mountain waldgeists? Do mountains really have waldgeists; do they create mirages? At the time there was little doubting a "yes" answer to both questions. Still, we slogged on.

We stopped every few steps, out of breath from the effects of both the altitude and cold, glanced at each other and smiled wanly. There was no turning back at this point. Finally, almost completely exhausted, we made it to the cabin minus one can of garden peas that we didn't find until the following summer about halfway up the incline from the place the ranger had dropped us off.

After searching for a while, we found the keys and stepped into the musty interior. As Kate began to unpack the groceries, I set about starting a fire in the fireplace. Then a stark reality slammed me right between my eyes! There was no wood; well, there were a few sticks, but nothing to sustain a fire. The family that used the cabin while we were overseas had not left any firewood, or if they had the dastardly gremlin had disposed of it. This was calamitous since the only source of heat was a fireplace, and it was really cold. We also had a small space heater, but alas, practically no Kerosene. The temperature was hovering in the teens, a precursor of things to come. Over the next few days the mercury dipped below zero, dropping to minus 6 degrees F. several nights. Had it not been for having an electric blanket and gasoline for our chainsaw, we might have given up and hiked off the mountain.

We opened the sofa bed in front of the fireplace, spread the electric blanket, and snuggled in for a cold night. Looking back, we shudder at the thought that had the electricity failed, we could possibly have frozen.

Next morning and each morning thereafter, we bundled up with the winter clothing that we had stored at the cabin. Looking much like North Pole denizens, we slogged through the snow to locate a standing dead tree. When we found a likely target, we sawed it down and dragged it back to the cabin to cut it into usable firewood. We would gather enough of the cut wood to keep a fire going throughout the remainder of the day and the following night. It was backbreaking work for a couple of city folk with mostly unused muscles just back from a two-year stint in semi-tropical Hong Kong, but it rekindled our atavistic spirit of survival that helped us to cope.

One of the chores that we faced during this particular very cold weather was to re-solder copper pipes that no matter how much precaution we took, still froze and popped joints. As I've mentioned, we get our water supply from a spring pumped overland through a flexible PVC pipe. It was so cold that the water in both the pump and the pipe froze overnight no matter what we did. Each morning after chopping firewood for the day, I slogged down the mountainside wielding a propane blowtorch to melt the ice in the pipe and pump.

Born out of the hatred for the daily chore, I finally thought of rigging a light bulb in the pump house and covering the pump with a blanket to trap the warmth from the bulb. That resolved the problem of the freezing pump, but not the one of the ice-clogged pipe; I still had to struggle down the 50-foot-long pipe with a torch each morning. Thawing the plastic pipe was tricky business; keeping the flame in one place too long meant a hole in the pipe, not long enough and the water inside remained frozen. . Looking back on the experience, we have two distinct thoughts: 1) what fools we were for venturing unprepared into the woods in the dead of winter and 2) despite the hard work, it was satisfying to have borne and overcome severe obstacles by our own hook.

We resolved that in the future, we would always maintain a store of firewood, plenty of gasoline for the chain saw, and Kerosene for the heater. During subsequent visits to the cabin in cool weather, we would bring the little one-burner heater out to take the chill off the cabin. During extreme cold, we started with heater in the morning until the wood fire could take over. Kate so loves warmth from the glowing ring of fire in the heater, she named it "ET". Only by an analyst's examination of her rationale can one understand why she relates the heater to the extra-terrestrial visitor in filmdom. It seems to have something to do with ET's glowing finger and the warm feeling created by the heater, or so she says. We recognize the danger of Kerosene heaters in closed spaces and take the precaution of cracking a window to allow oxygen to enter. Also, we never sleep with it burning and we don't leave it unattended at any time.

****

By this time, the reader will have realized that I, but not necessarily Kate, accept that there are woodland spirits, whether called waldgeists, ghosts, or gremlins; too many inexplicable events have occurred not to believe. Within a short time after we began using the property, I began to wonder what was causing the never-ending need for repairs, strange malfunctions of equipment, and even the unnatural noises we hear in the night. Kate and I have struggled with many challenges over the years ranging from the bothersome to the onerous, even to the dangerous. Looking back, many of the actions necessitated by these challenges are humorous in today's perspective, but they were most assuredly not so amusing at the time.

When the cabin was built, indoor water was transmitted through copper tubing, unlike the more modern PVC pipes. The major difference as far as maintenance and repairs go, is that copper tubing requires the use of solder, while the PVC is cemented. Consequently, repairs to the former are exceptionally more difficult. As mentioned earlier, the cabin has a very limited crawl space for servicing the apparatus installed there. Surely at least one gremlin lives in this space as there is a continual need to re-solder the pipes. The joint separations are most often caused by freezing, but that does not account for all the other times, hence my conclusion that it's the gremlin's doing.

Soldering pipes that are little more than 12-15 inches from the ground requires the talent of a contortionist to hold the joints together, hold the solder in place, and aim the propane torch. I still bear the scars from the hot solder dripping on me in any of various sites. Dripping hot solder is not the only problem. Since the pipes are by necessity close to the sub-flooring, wielding a blow-torch is a potential house fire hazard. Many joists bear the charred signature of the torch's blue flame. So, as you can see, repairing disjointed tubing, avoiding the dripping solder, extinguishing small fires caused by the blow-torch is not one of the humorous events.

One year, when we arrived for a summer-time stay, Kate noticed water coming from beneath the stack washer-dryer. She has always had an uncanny knack for finding even the tiniest of leaks. This one was easy to spot, as it had flooded the floor around the washer and seeped into the hall rug. I had to dismantle the washer to find the source of the leak. It turned out to be a small water diverter deep in the bowels of the machine. Water was leaking from a split seam. Even though I had winterized the cabin on our last visit, apparently a little water remained in the diverter causing it to freeze. Of course I had no replacement on the mountain, and when I phoned Sears for the part, I was informed that it was rare for such a part to cause problems and they did not stock it. By rushing the shipment they could have the plastic water diverter in a week or so. In the meantime, the gremlin was having a laughing fit as the water continuously leaked onto the floor and out into the hallway. We did not want to go a "week or so" unable to wash dirty clothes. So, in desperation I disconnected the water hose, removed the plastic part and using my electric glue gun, melted the seam together. It worked!

One year in March, my son-in-law and I decided to visit the cabin. (I've wondered many times why he chose to accompany me, as he is the antithesis of a jack-of-all-trades and definitely is not a mountain-man.) As noted before, the cabin has only the fireplace and a small Kerosene heater for warmth. The temperature was hovering in the twenties when we arrived.

Once I primed the pump, the water system seemed to be functioning despite the temperature. I built a fire and lit the space heater. After finally thawing my hands, frozen while cranking up of the water supply, I noticed the floor beneath the washer-dryer was wet. I suspected that it was the same problem I had faced before, but after Roy and I laboriously moved the stack washer-dryer so I could get behind it, I saw that the leak was from a copper tube joint resting against the wall that separated the washer room from the shower. I knew that soldering in such a tight spot would be tricky, thanks to gremlin's devious interferences, but I nevertheless put up a brave front before Roy. I broke out my solder and propane torch once again. This time I didn't need to lie on my back working on pipes just inches above my face, but I faced another challenge. The copper tubes abutted the wall with the plastic shower about three inches away. The poser was how I could heat the tubing enough to melt the solder without damaging the shower stall just millimeters away. Well, I couldn't. While the gremlin rested just above my head and smirked, I tried every trick I knew. I even placed a metal plate between the pipes and the shower wall. Despite my efforts, the shower stall bears the work of the gremlin to this day. The area where the pipe attaches to the shower knobs is gnarled and warped from the heat. I was lucky I didn't melt a hole in the plastic shower stall.

Copper pipes are not the only part of the plumbing that is subjected to the gremlins' tricks. At least four commodes have been replaced, by us or others using the cabin, because of cracks. Yes, we know that water should be drained from these conveniences before freezing weather, but thanks to the work of the gremlins, our efforts are not always successful. I have learned to replace the water in the commode with antifreeze. So far, we've not had to replace a toilet bowl for about five years. The frustrated gremlins have refocused their attention elsewhere.

The water supplying the cabin is pumped up from a cistern via an electric pump. When I constructed the reservoir, I also built a shelter for the pump to help protect it from falling debris and low temperatures However, the water must be drained from the pump if the temperature falls below 30 degrees and remains for several hours.

One year, the family visited the cabin in October and planned to return for the Thanksgiving holidays. Surely, we thought, there is no need to drain the water from the pump as it never freezes before December. We didn't account for the gremlins. When we arrived for our visit, the pump was frozen solid and the cast-iron housing was cracked. Cast iron cannot be welded. To mend the housing required a process called brazing. We had no backup so I spent all of one day searching for someone in town that could do brazing. I knew the gremlins were snickering at my efforts, so I decided to thwart their mischief by purchasing another pump to provide a spare. Though the gremlins have tried their tricks to disable the pump, swapping the faulty one for the spare has been relatively easy.

Other mischief the gremlins engage in includes clogging up the foot valve so that all the water drains back into the cistern as soon as the pressure reaches the gauge setting of 40 pounds per square inch. (Usual household pressure is 60 lb. per sq. in., but I haven't been able to achieve that with the setup we have.) The little green monsters can thereby keep the pump working overtime. Once, they caused the brass drive shaft between the motor and pump to shear in two, something that almost never happens under normal circumstances. A broken drive shaft is something that requires shop repair and part replacement. That's what prompted me to purchase a spare pump. It is a simple matter to replace the broken pump with the spare and take the broken one to the shop.

****

Brant and Deb have enjoyed the cabin over the years. While still teenagers, they fashioned large staffs both for hiking the mountain woods and for warding off the wild beasts of the forest they deemed it likely they would encounter. They explored all over Great North Mountain claiming finder's rights to special boulders, trees, and other unusual phenomena. Their favorite place was an outcropping of huge boulders that formed prominent cliffs along the top of the mountain. These behemoths, dating back to the Ice Age, were exposed when the local electric power company cleared the land beneath their lines. The granite and sandstone rocks were eventually bleached white by the elements. The kids named the outcropping, "The White Rocks", a name by which they have been known since.   When the kids stood on top of these great white rocks, the splendor of hundreds of square miles of mountains and forests spread out below them. With the wind blowing in their faces and the mountain birds singing, they could imagine themselves monarchs of the world looking down on their domain. When we accompanied them, we lingered to catch the splendiferous sunset as the great orb slowly settled behind the West Virginia hills; a splendid sight indeed!

Grandchildren Kevin, Lindsey, Alex, and Michelle followed in the footsteps of their parents. They too were captivated by the raw beauty of the scenario below them while standing atop the white rocks, as their parents had before them. Like their parents, the four youngsters discovered the nooks and crannies of the escarpment that runs along the top of the mountain and were fascinated by their exploration. Lindsey was not as enthusiastic as the others when it came to exploring the mountain top, most particularly she disliked entering the rock caves that could possibly be the home of spiders, lizards, snakes, and other disgusting creepy crawlers. Her preference was to find her own nook or cranny inside the cabin and curl up with a book.

Kevin, being the eldest of the boys, was the first of the grandchildren to explore the secrets of the escarpment. He climbed in and out of the boulders contorting his body to navigate the narrow crevices, risking scratches, bumps, falls, and possible encounters with the denizens of the rocky bluffs, particularly timber rattlers that also enjoyed the boulders. Later as he grew older and larger, he began to lose interest in navigating the tortuous passages, while Alex and Michelle's curiosity grew. Whenever any of the youngsters wound their way through the fissures and grottoes and onto boulders jutting out into the thin air overhanging the valley below, Granny Kate was a nervous wreck until she could account for everybody. Her concern was for me too, as I always preceded the exploration of the kids on these escapades. I was eternally grateful when their interest faded at the same time my bones and muscles began to rebel at the machinations required to negotiate the tight spaces. I must admit that I shared Brant's and Deb's enjoyment while exploring the rocks, but not so much as I got older while trying to keep up with the grandkids. .

In later years, I occasionally took the kids on camping trips along the spur trail the Appalachian Hiking Club constructed. While camped, we often hiked down the mountainside opposite our cabin to a permanent shelter for hikers and campers also built by the Club. We usually stopped by a hidden spring that seeps out from under an outcropping of huge rocks near the shelters. Except during dry spells, a cool drink of water could be coaxed from the spring. From the shelters, a trail leads past a shallow creek, known as Laurel Run, and on to a waterfall about a half mile farther. Except during draughts, when surface water was scarce, the waterfall was quite nice. Kate and I have often hiked to the waterfall and picnicked at the foot of the cascading water.

****

One time, on one of our frequent walks through the woods, this time in a different section of the mountain, we came upon a creek and followed it for some distance where we found a small one room cabin we had not known about before. The most unusual feature of this obviously very old cabin was that the owner had built a steel waterwheel and hooked up a small generator to it. The builder had diverted a flow of the stream to rotate the waterwheel and that generated a supply of direct current, to power a couple of light bulbs. Both the cabin and the waterwheel were in disrepair indicating the cabin had not been used for quite some time. We were intrigued by the cabin and its electricity supply and revisited it several times over the years, but have until this day seen no evidence of usage.

My sister and her son, Darrell, came for a visit one time and while there he decided to hike alone on the top of the mountain. We were aware that he was a city boy, with no experience in the wild, but felt that he was safe since, once on the mountain trails; all he need do to return home was walk downhill until reaching one of the roads that passed within sight of the cabin. But he stayed away so long that we became uneasy and tried to locate him. When we couldn't find any trace of him, our concern for his safety grew as we thought that perhaps he had been injured and was unable to walk. We had just about decided to call the sheriff's office for assistance when we received a phone call from a man asking if we were Darrel's relatives. It seems that the budding Daniel Boone had become disoriented on the top of the mountain and descended on the side opposite from the cabin. After wandering around for hours, he stopped at a cabin and asked for some water. The cabin resident recognized that Darrel was out of his element and after questioning him found that he had wandered more than five miles away from his starting point at our cabin and altogether had probably trekked more than ten miles! Darrel's benefactor met us on Back Creek road and we retrieved our lost explorer. Darrell claims that the mountain spirits misled him. And who am I to refute his claim?

****

Though the kids have given up crawling through the rocky labyrinth, Kate and I still go up with a picnic lunch and sit among the White Rock outcroppings for some quiet time. In recent years, we drive our four-wheeler up partway instead of hiking the all the way via the old Shawnee Indian trail and walk the last quarter mile to the top. We never tire of gazing over the valley between Virginia and West Virginia. This mountain and much of the surrounding territory was once the domain of Shawnee Indians. They were eventually pushed to the western side of the mountain, but continued to raid the settlers on the eastern side from time to time. After further subjugating the Indians, the Shawnee warpath created by the marauding bands was used by the Frye family to walk over the mountain to visit the settlements on the other side. The trail, though faint, still exists and now three generations of the Mercer family have trod this same path, though only to the top of the mountain, not down the other side. Sadly, now that the youngsters are older, interest in the Indian trail has faded. Even after more than thirty-eight years, Kate and I still walk a section of the warpath from time to time. Sometimes we can sense the spirits of the warriors as they hover among the trees that border the trail. Maybe these are the same spirits that play tricks on us from time to time and the same ones that led Darrell astray. After all, they were there millenniums before we interloped into their domain.

****

When Brant was a teenager, some of his friends from Cranbury, New Jersey, occasionally visited him at the cabin. They located wild grape vines hanging from tall trees, cut them loose near the ground and used the sturdy vines to swing out over the ravine. A miscalculation on these undertakings risked disastrous consequences from the rocks and debris in the ravine below. It was the kind of activity that Granny Kate preferred not to know about and certainly did not want to witness. As the boys swung into space, I just gritted my teeth and whispered a prayer. In reality, I wanted to follow their lead and swing into space as Johnny Weissmuller's Tarzan had done when I was a boy. Nowadays, nobody swings on the giant grape vines; probably just as well.

There was another pastime the kids used to enjoy near the original country home of Patsy Cline, the hugely successful country singer. Back Creek, at the foot of the mountain, rushes over some rocks across from the old dilapidated homestead of the Cline family. The surging water hollowed out some holes two or three feet deep. The kids and I constructed a rock dam that increased the depth to form a rudimentary swimming hole. On hot days, Kate and I would take whichever grand kids were visiting down to the makeshift swimming hole. The stream water was really cold all year and produced goose bumps on anyone dipping into the cold water, even on a hot summer's day.

The first time we used the swimming hole, we took Kevin and Lindsey. The youngsters had not brought bathing trunks, so they improvised. Kevin evinced little embarrassment as he stripped to his briefs. It's not that Kevin cannot be embarrassed, however, as I will comment on later. Lindsey resorted to wearing one of my tee-shirts that when wet caused a bit of consternation on her part. Later, when we took Alex and Michelle they had similar experiences, but Michelle best remembers the whistles from a couple of interested teenage boys hanging over the railing of a bridge crossing the creek twenty or so yards downstream. Alas, all the kids have lost interest in the rushing stream and our rudimentary swimming hole. And Kate was never the least bit interested in wading into the icy water.

Brant loved the woods and left his mark in numerous places. He laboriously hacked a trail from the cabin, past the old water supply and down the mountain to the main road. He had to cut bushes, downed trees that lay across his intended path, and move interfering rocks, but when finished, he had a nice cool footpath by which to wander down to where the streams from the two springs converge. Kevin has helped keep the path open over the subsequent years. There was another path that Kate and I developed in the early days at the cabin that led down the mountain from the opposite ravine and on to our closest neighbors.

Today, we can follow Brant's path, walk a little way up the main road then cut to this trail, past the present water supply back to the cabin. We usually stop at a leveled ground overlooking the spring where I had built a stone retaining wall, and placed a bench for resting and bird-watching. The flat surface, the gurgling stream, the canopy of trees and the comfortable bench make for a very pleasing spot.

Just recently Brant, Alex, Kate, and I laid a stone retaining wall alongside the stream up to the flattened area to keep the embankment from eroding. That project was a backbreaking task as we used very heavy fieldstone that had to be transported from the cabin area via a block and tackle setup to the spot beside the stream. Some of these stones weighed over 50 pounds.

Nowadays, we visit this spot for some cool spring water, picnic lunch and some interesting bird watching. Kate became interested in bird watching during a convalescent period in New York and has spent the past forty years identifying and recording birds found on the mountain and at home in Florida. To complement her hobby, I learned the process of identifying trees. I have since identified all the trees on our property. I treat these familiar trees as friends and often talk with them, making sure there are no humans within earshot, of course, because sometimes they talk back to me. Or is it the spirits of the long gone Shawnee Indians whispering.

Having outwitted the bears, raccoons, and squirrels, to keep them from eating all the birdfeed, Kate faced another challenge combating the yellowjackets that come up to dine on her hummingbird feeders. They also like to sample whatever we are eating or drinking while on the cabin deck. We often eat lunch there and usually have a plate of various fruits and melons.

The persistence of the yellowjackets is comical to me, well, Kate's reaction to them, but not to Kate. She chases the yellowjackets like a Visigoth wielding a battle axe, but in her case, yielding a flyswatter; she has worn out several of these weapons. She is scared of the little insects despite my sage advice that they don't arbitrarily sting people, only when they or their domain is threatened. Still, if one lands on the lip of one's glass to check out what the human is enjoying, the human has to avoid offending the bee accidentally, in which case the yellowjacket will strike back with its venom.

So Kate chasing around the deck swatting at the bees is a common sight most mid-summer days. So far, the bees haven't figured out that she is a deadly enemy that needs to be dealt with malice a forehand. She hasn't been stung since we stepped on their nest while searching for a spot for our cabin back in 1972, but she has a long memory. As cooler weather sets in, the yellowjackets become lethargic and soon disappear except for an occasional straggler. Finally Kate can relax, but not for long. For some strange reason we recently had to combat an infestation of "stink bugs". They settled in and on the cabin by the dozens. Out came Kate's trusty weapon, the fly swatter. She has swatted so many we have lost count, but they keep coming. I'm reasonably sure that the cabin gremlin has been at work keeping adversaries for Kate to battle. The stink bugs are very much akin to the gremlin's temperament.

****

Some people might see our sojourns to the cabin and our interaction with Father Nature's creatures as boring, but we have waited for over 38 years for boredom to set in. Other people would not like very much that we do not watch television, have no newspaper delivery, and do not even listen to the radio. Some years ago, I bought a computer for the cabin, mainly for my book writing chores, but I check the news blurbs on Google, and download emails. We read a lot, something we somehow don't seem to have time for at our Florida home. We also developed hobbies. Kate paints intricate designs on china which she "fires" in her own kiln while I do woodworking.

As mentioned before, we converted the smaller of the two bedrooms on the lower floor of the cabin into a kind of studio for Kate to paint, and installed a kiln for her to fire her work. I had a woodworking shop constructed behind the cabin.

A typical day for us at the cabin includes an early breakfast before Kate retreats to her studio; me to my woodworking shop. The *objet-d'arts* that Kate creates are usually given away as gifts as are the small animals that I carve. We have given gifts of our hobbies to people all over the world, recognizing that it is very difficult to find authentic American gifts for our overseas friends. Though our hobby output may not be as faultless as those of professionals, each gift carries with it a personal and unique characteristic.

****

There is an interesting phenomenon generally referred to as "left brain" or "right brain" domination and people tend to fall into one or the other of these designations. Although an over simplification, "left brain" refers to the use of analytical processes while "right brain" refers to creative processes. I love to take a block of wood and imagine a small animal or bird trapped inside it; then, whittle away the outside until the little animal emerges.

Kate spends hours hovering over her studio table reproducing trees, flowers, animals and birds on porcelain from images she has researched. To me, this is more analytical, but I hasten to add, Kate can be very creative as well as she puts her own stamp on the reproductions she paints.

Over the years, we have accumulated most of the accouterments of creature comfort for our cabin, including telephones, electric kitchen appliances (no dishwasher) a hot water heater, a rug to cover the plywood floor and various tools for obtaining firewood, keeping the immediate area around the cabin looking decent, and even a window air conditioner. At the outset, we installed overhead fans so that we can keep relatively cool during a rare hot spell. We have a television which we rarely switch on. The reception is so poor that watching the television is more a chore than entertainment anyway. Air conditioning and television are two of Kate's demons of civilization. It is only in a spell of unusual hot weather that the air conditioner is needed anyway. We both try to avoid the "noise" of civilization, preferring the sounds of the forest. After all, we reason, that's why we bought the property and built the cabin. At night, we hear the nocturnal animals moving about; in the late summer, we are serenaded by the cicadas and katydids.

In recent years, though buffered by the seven acres surrounding the cabin, we can now hear distracting sounds of civilization from other families that occupy several cabins built over the years. The most annoying noises are the ATVs. Despite the fact that the land is private property and the roads are reserved, these noisy vehicles invade the mountain from time to time. Aside from the noise, these pesky demons destroy the mountain trails.

Some of the people joining us on the mountain have been less desirable than others. One real character moved into a cabin on a road we frequently walked. His place was about a mile from us. He began collecting scrap cars and other rubbish until his yard looked like a junkyard. He also dumped used motor oil on his property. Neighbors asked the county EPA agents to have the reprobate cease and desist, but he was a real curmudgeon and used a varied vocabulary of vulgar and offensive words whenever confronted particularly by the EPA agents. Under pressure from the authorities, he promised to move the junk and stop dumping used oil, but he continued as usual. Then one day someone noticed his dogs were howling and appeared to be hungry. A friend and neighbor investigated and found the man had died, apparently quite some time before. The man was a colorful albeit obnoxious character, and while we could not help but feel relieved that he no longer was contaminating our beloved mountain with either his junk or his vocabulary, we felt saddened that he died alone.

A couple close to our place with whom we had become friends sold their cabin and left the mountain. The place changed hands several times before another man with curmudgeon traits moved in, and to the consternation of others on the mountain had all but one or two trees on his property sawed down. Along with others, we wondered why someone would buy a cabin to enjoy the woods, and then denude his property. Oddly, this man also died while alone and was discovered by his son sometime later.

There have been several colorful characters that found a home on Great North Mountain, but we've no inclination to write about them; except for one. Neil Miller, a true mountain-man, built a fine home down the mountain a ways. He is a retired tool and dye engineer and owns many kinds of equipment. He enjoys operating massive roadwork machines with which he has maintained the roads for several years. A few grateful property owners donate funds periodically to Mr. Miller, but unfortunately others simply enjoy his largesse without contributing funds.

Luckily, we have not been bothered by burglars or other undesirables, probably because of the difficulty navigating the roads and because there is only one way back off the mountain. We did have a burglary once that took items that were easily transported and then sold at yard sales. Since we had never been burgled by anyone before, we concluded that the job was done by a group of rather strange people temporarily staying down the mountain. The burglars apparently camped in the cabin for some time before taking items they could carry before leaving. Oddly, even though they apparently searched the cabin carefully, they replaced almost everything they didn't want back where they had found it. Since the place was not ransacked, and only small items were taken, the investigating deputy sheriff commented that the burglary was a non-professional job; if it had been conducted by professionals, they would have "cleaned you out." Thankfully, the loss was covered by our insurance policy. We've had no more problems of unwanted visitors since that episode.

Kate and I can remember the early years and how difficult it was to reach our cabin on the old unimproved, poorly maintained roads, especially in rainy or snowy weather. The upper reaches of the old road has a steep hill, that we aptly named "chicken hill" because when some viewed the incline they sometimes "chickened out" before attempting the climb. On numerous occasions our car would spin out halfway up the incline. One time in particular is indelibly imprinted on my memory. Kate's folks had finally accepted our invitation to visit our refuge. On the day of their arrival it rained, so we parked their car at the bottom of the mountain and proceeded in our sedan, hoping that somehow we could maneuver it up chicken hill in the rain. It was not to be however. When we reached midpoint of the hill, made extremely slippery by the downpour, we stalled. Continuing up was impossible and retracing our assent was precarious, so I blocked the car with stones to prevent it from sliding down hill, jacked up first one wheel, and then the other and installed the heavy duty chains we kept for emergencies. This effort was conducted in a heavy rain while desperately trying to maintain my footage on the muddy hillside. My mother-in-law sat inside the vehicle outwardly stoically, but I knew she was building a case to support her belief that her daughter had married a miscreant. I was not her favorite son-in-law. Actually, I was her only son-in-law.

For many years we had the annoying task of accumulating our soiled clothing, taking the bundle to a Laundromat in town, and waiting for the washing and drying. Kate, of course, was not very happy with that arrangement, so we purchased a Sears stack washer/dryer. The only place we could find to put the appliance without the ugliness of having the devices on our deck was in the closet where the water heater was installed. This meant that we had to relocate the water tank. Despite our careful measurement, when the laundry unit was delivered it would not fit into the closet and allow the door to close. So, the project (as usual with interference with our gremlin) turned out to be more complicated than we imagined at first. Brant and I had to extend the door facing about six inches so we could install folding louvered doors. That did the trick and didn't look unsightly. Mission accomplished; gremlin outwitted once again!

Of course, we didn't want to do without hot water. After removing the old water heater, we purchased a new one and installed it in the crawl space beneath the cabin floor near where we had already installed a cold water tank. Because of the low clearance, we had to dig a hole in which to place the tank, run an electric power line to the unit, and install copper tubing to connect the hot water to the cabin system. This was not without a great deal of toil, sweat, inhalation of dust and, according to Kate, a profusion of "unacceptable language". The work had to be done kneeling, crawling or lying flat on our stomachs, all the while keeping a wary eye out for the gremlin that we knew lived with other creatures that love the dark recesses of the crawl space. The area below the floor ranges from about six inches to about 30 inches high.

Brant has continued to help with various projects that would have been very nearly impossible without him; but I must give Kate credit. For a 105 pound five-foot tall aging lady, she does a phenomenal job on many projects.

When the cabin was built, I requested triple insulation to protect against the mountain cold. The floor was insulated with six inches of fiberglass, but unfortunately, the wood mice found this very convenient for raising their broods, causing an unsightly mess and a less than savory odor. Eventually, Brant and I got up enough courage to crawl under the cabin and tear out this insulation, mice nests and all. He wriggled along on his stomach pulling the nasty stuff down while I followed along and dragged it to the outside. We have done many projects together, but this was indubitably the nastiest and the scariest. We had no idea what varmints we might run into living in the insulation, but we were lucky and escaped unscathed except for the dust, fiberglass filaments, and mice leavings that we breathed.

During the years that Lindsey came up she spent most of her time reading, but she did find time to become interested in a teenage boy who lived down the mountain. On one of the visits she ventured too close to the chained family dog which promptly bit Lindsey on her tush. Since the dog remained chained, where it could be watched for possible rabies, we did not take Lindsey to the emergency room for anti-rabies injections, but attended to her wounds ourselves. Being a teenager, Lindsey was very chagrined at having to show her behind to us for treatment notwithstanding the fact that Kate and I had changed her diapers when she was a baby.

This same dog attacked Alex later on when he was about five years old. He, along with the rest of the family, walked down to visit the neighbors and as we were standing around talking, the dog emerged from the woods caring a dead puppy in her mouth. Suddenly, she dropped the puppy and attacked Alex. Deb and I shielded Alex between us, but despite our efforts the dog managed to bite Alex several times and only stopped when the dog's owner managed to pull it off. I'm sure a dog psychologist could explain why she picked Alex from the small crowd to attack, but we could never figure it out.

Later, the dog's owner, shocked and greatly distressed at the dog's actions, tracked the half-wild animal to her lair and shot her thereby unwittingly forcing Alex to get rabies shots. It seems that if an animal cannot be contained and observed or examined immediately upon death there is no way it can be determined if rabies is present. We were not aware of this requirement. The initial treatment in the emergency room at the Winchester hospital cost $400, and continued treatments ran into the thousands.

When we were overseas, the family that used and took care of the cabin had a son in the paint store business. He convinced his dad, Wilton that the cabin deck needed to be sanded and painted with a waterproof paint. Wilton contacted me in Hong Kong and I agreed to pay the $400 bill. Mistake! The waterproof paint trapped moisture and allowed the huge carpenter ants to eat away at the wood without appearing on the surface. Within a couple of years, the deck was a mess. Brant came to the rescue again. I ordered new treated lumber and we took the old deck down and installed a new one along with a new landing—a big job!

The grandchildren took a great interest in spending time at the cabin in their early years, but as is the way of teenagers, they spend less and less time here. I can remember teaching Kevin how to chop firewood, weed-whack the yard and to use various tools in my shop. Lindsey, on the other hand, was never a "woodsy" type person. She has always been happy reading for hours and that is the practice she pursued during her many stays at the cabin. Kate gave Lindsey some firsthand lessons on housecleaning, however, much to the teen's discomfiture.

One endearing and comical experience with Kevin deserves mentioning. As a teenager, he was a voracious eater. When he visited, we never had leftovers—he ate everything. One evening while we were dining on Granny Kate's outstanding spaghetti and meat sauce, Kevin replenished his plate while Kate and I were still at the table on the porch. As Kevin stepped down from the cabin floor to the porch, he tripped. The full plate of spaghetti and meat sauce sailed through the air like a missile from outer space and plopped on the floor in a viscous mass. While Kate and I were contorted in laughter, Kevin was totally embarrassed and apologetic. The only negative thing of the episode was that there was no more spaghetti.

Deb's children, Alex and Michelle were also enthusiastic about spending time at the cabin. When they came to the cabin Kate and I encouraged pursuits not readily available at their home. Michelle did some painting under Kate's tutelage and both she and Alex have undertaken numerous projects with me, some of which provided them with training for future use. They readily took to these projects, and Alex in particular liked woodworking, especially carving, and has turned out some excellent work. Michelle also carved a couple of animals as well.

Alex has also picked up skills in plumbing, electricity, and stonework. He listens to my instructions and is a quick learner. One time, however, Alex did not heed instructions. He was helping me clean underbrush from around the overland PVC water pipe. Alex was wielding a machete while I used a garden hoe. I cautioned him to be very careful as he could damage the plastic pipe with the machete. The warning words had no sooner left my lips, when with a mighty swoosh, he chopped a gash in the pipe causing the pressured water to shoot twenty feet into the air. I was not overly complimentary on his actions, shouting a few words he had not heard me use before, however Kate thought the whole affair was hysterical.

I patched the cut with no serious consequences. Alex has retained a vivid memory of this incident. Other projects Alex undertook under my watchful eye included: the installation of electrical wire from the connection on the porch across the ceiling and down the wall to provide for an outlet to my computer. He replaced the screens on the porch and did considerable re-painting. The chimney needed some caulking so Alex climbed atop the stone monolith while I held to a rope tied around his waist. There wasn't really much danger of him falling, but we didn't want to take a chance as he was over twenty feet above the ground. We both wondered what his mom would have said had she seen him twenty-two feet up tethered by a rope around his waist. Granny Kate was a nervous wreck. Brant has also made similar repairs in a similar fashion.

Alex always had a project in mind when he arrived. Although I found some of them a bit strange (items he gleaned from various fantasy TV shows, I think). They suited him so that is what we worked on. Kevin also learned a good bit about woodworking and how to use the tools as well. One of Kevin's projects on the jigsaw still hangs over Kate's dressing table.

****

As I've written earlier, Kate and I have many "battles" with local fauna. A few years ago, our efforts turned to mourning doves that swoop in and clean out all the birdfeeders they can enter. We have a couple of finch feeders enclosed in wire that thwart them. I don't seem to win the majority of these battles, but I valiantly keep up the resistance much to Kate's amusement. I even fashioned a sling shot from a branch and shoot small pebbles at the doves. My aim is such that the doves are quite safe from harm, but it usually scares them away for a while. Kate laughs continuously as I fire my supply of pebbles, gather more and do the same. Never once have I hit one of the pesky birds.

Sometimes being in the woods when all is quiet and dark gets a little spooky. Strange noises tend to prey on one's nerves. Being a natural prankster, a trait I inherited from my dad, I built what the folks in and around my birthplace in Alabama call a "dumbbull". I have no clue as to the derivation of that name. In the old days, according to my late parents, mischievous boys would stretch a cow hide over a barrel and attach a rope smeared with resin in the center of the hide. When the boys pulled on the resin dipped rope the hide reverberated with a sound similar to a roar of a bear. Reputedly, the noise was so frightening that farm animals sometimes broke out of their stalls and headed for the hills. The dumbbull that I created was not so grandiose; it was made of a pasteboard oatmeal box and a string dipped in Kerosene. When I pulled on the string it made a completely unidentifiable noise that was in fact a bit unnerving. Kate, Brant and the grandkids liked to play board games on the porch during the evening; I didn't. I quickly became a persona-non-grata after sneaking up on them and sounding the dumbbull just outside the screen window. The women squealed and Brant nearly jumped out of his skin. Once I owned up to being the culprit, I made a dumbbull for the grandkids. However, after about an hour of them generating the eerie noise, it became evident that it had not been such a good idea. I wondered what the gremlin thought of the eerie noise, probably wished he had a dumbbull.

It was usually easy to frighten our kids and later the grandkids who liked to go on camping trips when they were small. I used to tell them a story I made up about an old yellow hand that inhabited the woods. The gist of the story was that the disembodied, shriveled hand, yellowed with age was that of Baron Goranovich, a cruel and despotic ruler of a small fiefdom in Transylvania. It was a tall tale that had the severed hand resting in formaldehyde for 200 years before somehow finding its way to Great North Mountain. Later on, I captured the tale in a book I wrote entitled, "The Old Yellow Hand".

According to legend, the gruesome old hand roamed the environs of the mountain wreaking revenge on any human it came across while searching for its master's body.

The common rustling noises always present in the forest at night were attributed to the hand as it crawled among the leaves and other woodland debris surrounding the campsites. Making up new episodes for the yarn each time I retold it on recurring camping trips was challenging and highly amusing to me. I had to be careful to preserve the primary storyline or risk the kid's trust in my infallibility.

Of all the grandchildren, Alex seemed particularly vulnerable to scary tales. When very young, he seemed to have a greater fear of dark woods and noises than the other grandkids. He feared "the monkey in the trees". Nobody knows how his fear got started. I carved a gruesome mask from a pine knot and hung it on a tree near the entrance to the cabin yard. He became accustomed to it and seemed to get over his fear. The mask is still in its place and Alex hasn't forgotten it. He is fearless in the woods now.

Michelle was a bit more sangfroid, but was still vulnerable to the horror factor of my stories. Alex had a friend sleepover and I took them camping on top of the mountain. Michelle wanted to go, but the boys strictly forbade the presence of a girl. I promised her that I would take her camping another time. A week or so later she and I camped at a lovely site on a rocky embankment surrounded on three sides by a second growth of birch trees. These young trees made a particularly soothing sound to me, but Michelle had different feelings about the "weird" sounds.

When I told the tale of the old yellow hand that evening, I of course incorporated the soughing in the treetops and the rustling of mice in fallen leaves. As ever, she paid rapt attention to my recounting of the oft-told story about the treacherous old hand. As we stared into the dying embers of campfire, the usual nighttime noises became scarier and scarier to Michelle. She was already inside her sleeping bag although still outside the tent. As the suspense heightened, she sank deeper and deeper into the sleeping bag. When I reached the end of this particular episode, I scuttled the remaining campfire embers and we moved to the safety of the tent. Michelle literally jumped into her sleeping bag again and zipped it up all the way completely covering her entire body including her head. She could still hear the old yellow hand scurrying about in the dry leaves outside the tent prompting her to unzip the bag part way every few minutes all night long, pop her head out and whisper, "What was that papa?", Then she begged me to confirm that we were safe from the clutches of the terrible old hand. After two or three hours, sleepiness overcame her fear of the unidentifiable sounds and she slumbered peacefully until morning.

Lindsey preferred a good book in the comfort of the cabin than sleeping on the hard ground, fighting off flying pests of the night, and dealing with the sounds of withered old yellow hands roaming around where she was sleeping.

For that reason, Kate made her a snug retreat in a room by herself so she could enjoy her reading without interruption.

****

After many frustrating years of navigating the steep hill to our cabin with our family sedan, we purchased a Mazda pickup truck. Though it was not the ideal solution, it relieved our town car of the arduous up and down trips. But again the pesky gremlin went to work. While we spent the winter in Florida, the gremlin led the mountain field mice to a refuge in the parked vehicle. When we returned the following summer, we could smell the stench of months of mouse excrement emanating from the entrance holes in the plastic headliner, so we decided it was time to retire the Mazda for a 4-wheel drive Ford SUV. The little mice also found the inside of the cabin a comforting respite from the cold winter. We found their nests, and sometimes their young, in various places. We set mousetraps all over the cabin and caught dozens of the little rodents over the years. We also use insect bombs to discourage their return. So far, so good.

I would be remiss if I did not revisit one of the great challenges extant at our refuge. Early on, as I've mentioned, the roads were virtually impassable in the rain or snow. In later years, we had a road builder construct another passage that followed the old Shawnee Trail up some distance then curved off at the first relatively flat area. The new road eliminated the necessity of challenging Chicken Hill. Unfortunately, the first rise in the new road is hard to navigate in the rain because of an accumulation of kaolin clay; the same deposit from which I dug enough to stem the flow of water in the construction of the cistern. The deposit is at the crest of the first steep part of the new road. When a rain wets this clay, it becomes a gooey, slippery mess causing spin-outs when trying to climb the hill.

The continuing challenge of the roads led to the realization that we needed a more rugged vehicle than the family sedan or the two-wheel drive Mazda. We bought a series of mountain vehicles after the Mazda pickup truck, first, a Ford Explorer, then a Chevrolet Blazer, and a Pontiac Aztec. Once we were able to get up the hill in our Florida vehicle, it was parked for the summer. I built a carport attached to the workshop for this vehicle. Though certainly not a skilled carpenter, the carport turned out fairly well, but the gremlin patiently waited a chance to interfere. We had a truck deliver some material to the cabin, but once ready to leave, the driver could not turn the vehicle around in the small space left after building the carport. To rescue the truck, I had to remove one post holding up the roof to allow room for the truck to maneuver a turn-around. Of course, with the nasty little trickster perched on the carport roof smirking, I had to jack up the corner of the shelter and replace the post I had removed.

The one good thing about the rugged roads leading up to the mountain is that it's so intimidating to the casual wayfarer bent on hiking or driving to the top of the mountain that they rarely appear on the mountain. The various service vehicles, such as the telephone company truck and the meter reader manage to cope, but the UPS and FedEx drivers won't risk damage to their trucks trying to climb to the cabin. They leave any packages for us with the neighbors at the bottom of the mountain.

Still in a small way, I miss the challenge of the old roads and the goose-pimples I used to have on Chicken Hill when our car was mired in mud and gradually slipping backwards down the mountain before I could install the heavy duty chains I kept in the trunk. Kate is quite happy however, and has no regrets for leaving that excitement behind.

****

Grandson Alex is an adventuresome young man. He expressed an interest in going canoeing one summer, so I researched likely rivers that would not be overly challenging or too placid. When he, his sister Michelle and his mom Deb came to the cabin afterwards, we set out on our great adventure. We intended to canoe down the chosen river for several hours and camp on the bank. We loaded all our equipment in two canoes, Alex and Michelle in one and Deb and I in the other. Off we went—but a much slower pace than we planned on. The river was at its lowest level in a decade and it was impossible to steer over and around the many rocks that would have been submerged in higher water times. The slow current and the obstacles often prevented us from floating free, instead we had to paddle or portage almost all the way.

After several tiring hours, we pulled up to inspect a campsite only to find that it and the next two we looked at were unsuitable in every aspect.

Exasperated, we decided to forego camping and proceed to our ultimate pickup site. We telephoned the vendor to meet us there that evening, not to wait until the next day. The pickup van arrived just before nightfall and we returned to our starting point.

Needless to say, the canoeing trip was a bust. The vendor would refund only a small portion of the original fee paid, adding to my dissatisfaction with the way the venture turned out. And the episode put a damper on future such trips. We resolved to make sure of an adequate water level before considering future canoeing trips.

Alex had equipped himself with the latest camping paraphernalia for our canoeing trip and was anxious to try out his new equipment, so he and I went on a camping trip in the Shenandoah National Park, he in his one-man tent and I in our family tent. His modern camping gear performed quite well when preparing a meal or coffee. The park is very people friendly and the campsites well kept. Animals roamed freely among the campers. We both enjoyed our outing.

Kate expressed an interest in camping in the park after hearing my favorable report on Alex's and my trip. I arranged for a trip for just the two of us and thoroughly enjoyed our overnight stay. Kate particularly loved the tameness of the deer that wandered into our campsite.

****

A few years ago I purchased a computer to read the news, check the weather, keep in contact with family and friends, and especially for my latest pastime, writing   I tried to obtain a wireless connection to the Internet, but several attempts by vendors failed.   First we invited a couple of satellite providers to try for a signal; the first simply said it wasn't possible to get a signal. The other tried more diligently, but finally declared that I'd have to cut down several trees that were interfering with the satellite signal. Next, I tried a connection using signals broadcast from a tower on top of the mountain, but that failed because the tower uses line-of-sight for connections and the signal passed over the cabin.

Finally, I tried Verizon's wireless network. But after many hours spent with the Verizon tech support we gave up on that source as well. The process uses the same signals as cell phones and the signal strength is rarely more than the minimal two-bars on the phone indicator. That strength is insufficient to power Internet connections consistently, and besides almost anything such as airplanes, high winds, storms, etc., interrupted the signal. The only connection that works is land-line telephone. Of course that ties up the telephone line and prevents its use for incoming and outgoing calls.

The connection speed is extremely slow by today's standards, so I have to avoid both emails and web sites where large downloads are involved. Since we are on the end of the phone lines, we lose connection often, particularly during high winds that continually drop limbs and or trees across the lines below us. The transition from high speed cable in Florida to snail-like dial-up on the mountain is exasperating.

The slow connection speed does not interfere with my book writing efforts since it is done off-line, so all is not lost. A Cabin on the Mountain was my first book written in the summer of 2000. Five more followed over the subsequent years. The original version was published by a publisher that maintained all rights for seven years. Now that seven years have passed, I decided to re-write the book to include the many adventures that have occurred since that book's publication. This revised version is entitled A Cabin on Great North Mountain,

****

Nowadays, partly thanks to the improved roads, we leave the mountain for the surrounding towns and villages much more than we did in the past. One reason is that cooking for two people has become a low return on Kate's investment of time. Gone are the delightful homemade biscuits, deep-dish pies, teacakes, and other culinary delights of the past.

First, as I've mentioned, the roads are much more navigable, second, our aging metabolism can't handle the calories anymore, and third, there are many new restaurants that cater especially to the latest trend of away-from-home dining. Country style meals in small West Virginia and Virginia villages are special treats. The largest town in our area, Winchester, boasts almost any cuisine one could want. We especially like the Mexican and Indian restaurants, but often go to the American style pubs for a beer or two and whatever their bar menus offer.

****

Kate and I have been married for 57 years at this writing, and luckily we are good friends so we can pass the time on the mountain, just the two of us, hardly noticing that a week or month has slipped by. Since retirement, we usually stay all summer, and sometimes the early fall months as well. As mentioned before, she spends a lot of time in her studio painting on porcelain, but never neglecting her passion, bird watching. I still make a lot of sawdust in my woodworking shop, but not as much as in the past. Writing has encroached on my woodworking projects. When we add the occasional mountain hikes, we lead quite a full life. Even so, we still occasionally take a break from this routine more so than in the past to visit other scenic places such as the Shenandoah National Park high in the Blue Ridge Mountains, Blackwater Falls State Park in West Virginia and others.

We hope that this account of the family's experiences on Great North Mountain will be source for interesting reading for the generations that follow us.

Kate and Earnest Mercer, 2012

End

Earnest and Kate Mercer